Hermogenes'
On Types of Style

HERMOGENES'

On Types of Style

Translated by Cecil W. Wooten

The University of North Carolina Press

Chapel Hill and London

Library of Congress Cataloging-in-Publication Data

Hermogenes, 2nd cent.

  Hermogenes' on types of style.

  Translation of: Peri ideōn.

  1. Rhetoric, Ancient.   2. Style, Literary.   I. Title.

II. Title: On types of style.

PA3998.H8E5   1987   808   86-24954

ISBN 0-8078-1728-7

For My Father and

Billie Jean

Contents

Preface

I did the first draft of this translation when I was a fellow at the National Humanities Center during the fall of 1980 and the spring of 1981, and I am grateful to the National Endowment for the Humanities and the American Council of Learned Societies for providing the grants that made that year possible. Another grant from the University Research Council of the University of North Carolina at Chapel Hill aided in the publication of this work, and I gratefully acknowledge the council's generous support. I am also extremely grateful to George Kennedy, who first introduced me to Hermogenes and encouraged at every turn my efforts to do a publishable translation of this treatise. He carefully read the first draft of the manuscript and made many valuable suggestions on it. I would also like to thank Donald Russell, whose very careful and thorough reading of the translation saved me from many potentially embarrassing errors and many awkward turns of phrase. And I am indebted to George Kustas, who also read the work and made valuable comments on it. Checking a translation can be a very tedious task, and I am consequently all the more grateful to these three scholars for the generosity with which they have shared with me their knowledge and their expertise. Finally, I would like to thank Laura S. Oaks, who copyedited the text for The University of North Carolina Press.

Chapel Hill, 1986

Introduction

Hermogenes of Tarsus is said to have been a child prodigy whose oratorical skill was so widely known that when he was fifteen he was visited by the emperor Marcus Aurelius, who came to hear him speak when he toured the eastern provinces (Philostratus 2.577). Since we know that Marcus Aurelius was in the East in A.D. 176, this would put Hermogenes' birth around 161. His oratorical abilities, however, seem to have declined soon after the emperor's visit, and Hermogenes may have turned to the writing of rhetorical treatises. Five survive under his name, and according to ancient authorities they were all written before he was twenty-three. The *Progymnasmata*, which consists of short descriptions of preliminary exercises in rhetorical composition, may not be by Hermogenes; *On the Method of Force* is surely spurious. The one book *On Staseis* is clearly genuine, but the four books *On Invention* are more doubtful. However, the longest, most interesting, and most influential of his works is the treatise *On Types of Style*, in two books, which is surely authentic.

In this work Hermogenes outlines, with almost mathematical precision, seven basic types or ideal forms of style: Clarity, Grandeur, Beauty, Rapidity, Character, Sincerity, and Force (*saphēneia, megethos, kallos, gorgotēs, ēthos, alētheia,* and *deinotēs*).[1] Since some of these types can be broken down into subtypes, it would be more accurate to say that Hermogenes describes twenty basic types of style. He conducts his discussion by considering each type or subtype in terms of the various elements out of which speech is created. These he sees as being thought or content (*ennoia*); approach (*methodos*),[2] which he eventually identifies with figures of thought; and style (*lexis*), which is concerned with choice of diction, figures of speech, clauses, word order, cadences, and rhythm. By combining these basic elements in various ways an orator can produce the many types of style that Hermogenes describes.

Hermogenes' exposition is very systematic, but it is also complicated. To give the reader some guidance let me briefly outline the whole system. Hermogenes realized that the most basic requirement of any speech is that it be clear, and the first type of style that he discusses, therefore, is Clarity (*saphēneia*). His discussion of Clarity (Rabe 226–241; see num-

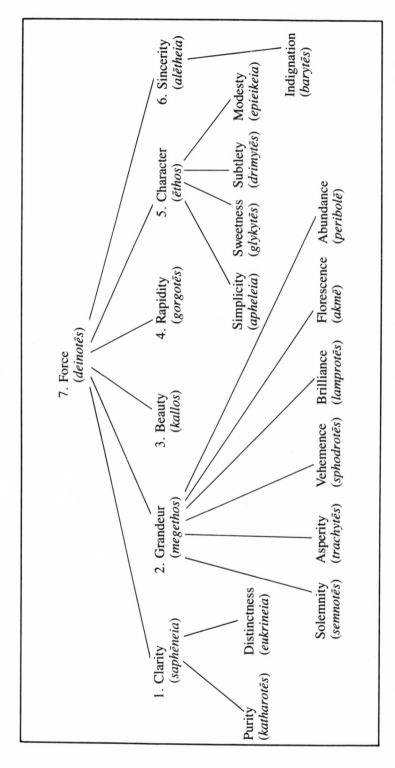

Hermogenes' Types and Subtypes of Style

bers at margins in this translation) is divided into two parts, Purity (*katharotēs*), which is concerned with the sentence itself, and Distinctness (*eukrineia*), whose goal is to make the whole speech clear.

The thought of a clear sentence must be one that is familiar to most people. It must be expressed in a conversational manner, as a direct statement of fact, using clauses that are short and complete in themselves and simple structures consisting of a subject in the nominative case and a main verb. The clauses should employ the loose rhythms of conversation, especially iambs. These recommendations, with which Hermogenes deals under the rubric of Purity, will make a sentence clear.

Under Distinctness Hermogenes deals with techniques of making the speech as a whole clear. He recommends that the orator state clearly what he will say and how he will develop his arguments, and make his transitions from one thought to the next clear and smooth, often using summaries of what he has already said and repeating his basic organizational principle.

Hermogenes realized that a speech that is extremely clear runs the risk of appearing to be trite, commonplace, or obvious. In his discussion of Grandeur (*megethos*) he therefore deals with the various ways in which an orator can keep the clear from appearing to be mundane. He divides Grandeur into six subtypes. These, however, can here be arranged into three basic units: Solemnity and Brilliance; Abundance; and Asperity, Vehemence, and Florescence.

The thoughts characteristic of Solemnity (*semnotēs*) are general, universal statements about elevated topics such as justice, goodness, and glorious deeds. The thought must be stated directly, without hesitation or qualification, using short clauses and a preponderance of nouns rather than verbs. The use of long syllables and diphthongs will further increase the dignity of the sentence (242–254). Brilliance (*lamprotēs*) is similar to Solemnity, except that the thought is somewhat different. Brilliance should be used when the orator is describing a noble act, but one that is of somewhat less universal import than those glorious deeds that are dealt with under Solemnity. Demosthenes, for example, might describe his efforts to effect an alliance between Athens and Thebes in a brilliant way, but the defeat of the Persians at Salamis would be described in a solemn manner. The style of Brilliance is similar to that of Solemnity, except that the clauses are often longer and expansive rather than compact (262–269).

Amplification or Abundance (*peribolē*) is the second major component of Grandeur. Synonymity, enumeration, polysyndeton, and other expansive devices can be used to give emphasis and greater import to a thought. Abundance, like Solemnity and Brilliance, can make a clear thought vivid and lift it above the commonplace (277–296).

The third subtype of Grandeur is composed of Asperity (*trachytēs*), Vehemence (*sphodrotēs*), and Florescence (*akmē*). These keep a speech from appearing mundane by injecting an element of passion, especially anger, into certain passages. All these types are used when the orator wants to reproach a rival and to give his speech an air of spontaneity that reflects his own anger or impatience. Asperity (254–260) is used when the orator criticizes a person or group that is more important than himself. The style is fairly harsh, using short, choppy clauses, simple phrases, sounds that clash, and figurative language. (In the translation I have consistently used *harsh* to denote adjective forms of *trachytēs*.) Exclamations and rhetorical questions can be especially effective in conveying the orator's own emotions. Vehemence (260–264) is used against a person or group considered to be inferior to the orator. Here there is no mitigation whatsoever of the criticism, which is made more openly and more sharply than in Asperity. Florescence (269–277) is the opposite of Vehemence. It should be used when the orator wants to make his accusations in a somewhat gentler manner. By using longer clauses and those figures of speech, such as anaphora, that are often associated with poetry and that consequently give a pleasing effect, the orator can soften his reproach and make his criticism in a less harsh way.

The poetic figures of speech that are used in Florescence can also be used in greater profusion in other passages to charm and delight the audience with language that is, above all, pleasing to hear. Hermogenes deals with this aspect of speech in the next type of style that he discusses, which he calls Beauty (*kallos*) (296–311). Beautiful language tends to relax the tone of the speech, to soften its intensity. It should be used when the orator wants to beguile his audience or to distract them from the content of his speech.

Sometimes, however, the orator will want, not to distend, but to compress his argument and to sketch out a point as quickly as possible. This gives energy and vivacity to the speech and can be used to convey to the audience the impatience or excitement that the orator himself feels. Hermogenes treats this type of style under the rubric of Rapidity (*gorgotēs*) (312–320). This type of style is characterized by short questions, rapid replies, sharp and quick antitheses, and extremely short, choppy sentences. The predominant rhythm is trochaic.

The fifth type of style that Hermogenes treats, Character (*ēthos*), is really a type of argument more than a style. It is made up of several styles, most of which are similar to those that have already been discussed, whose basic goal is to exhibit the orator's character in such a way as to win the goodwill of the audience. In other words, what Hermogenes calls Character is simply a collection of approaches whose basic goal is to effect what Aristotle in the *Rhetoric* (1.2.4.) calls the "ethical appeal."

Simplicity (*apheleia*) (322–329) is the first of these approaches that Hermogenes discusses. Simplicity is similar to Clarity, but its purpose is not simply to be clear but also to persuade the audience that the orator is the sort of person who can perceive complex issues and explain them in a clear and comprehensible way—which wins him the goodwill, respect, and trust of his hearers.

In addition to Simplicity Hermogenes treats under Character three other styles that help the orator to win the goodwill of his audience: Sweetness (*glykytēs*) (330–339), Subtlety (*drimytēs*) (339–345), and Modesty (*epieikeia*) (345–352). Sweetness is like Beauty in that it delights the audience by injecting poetic devices into the speech. But Sweetness is even more intensely poetic than Beauty and uses elements of poetry that are not generally considered to be characteristic of oratory. Under Subtlety Hermogenes deals with techniques through which an orator can express himself in especially clever and striking ways in order to impress the audience with his intelligence. Under the rubric of Modesty he treats approaches that help the orator to persuade his audience that he is basically humble and unpretentious, so that they will more readily sympathize with him.

Verity or Sincerity (*alētheia*) (352–368), Hermogenes' sixth type of style, is similar to Character in that it teaches the orator how to project an image of "one plain-dealing man addressing another in whose judgment he has perfect confidence."[3] Prayers, oaths, anacolutha, sudden reproaches, and exclamations convey Sincerity by giving the audience the impression that the orator has been suddenly moved by great emotion and is speaking more or less extemporaneously. These seemingly spontaneous outbursts must be introduced without transition or preparation, so that they will not appear to have been prepared in advance. Figures of speech such as apostrophe, diaporesis, correctio, parentheses, and unfinished enumerations also give the impression that the orator is speaking spontaneously; and short clauses and uneven rhythms, which Hermogenes has also associated with Vehemence, can be used to convey the orator's emotion. Indignation (*barytēs*) (364–368), a subtype of Sincerity, involves the use of irony, which cannot be successful unless a frank and candid relationship exists between the speaker and his audience.

Gravity or Force (*deinotēs*) (368–380), the seventh type of style, is really nothing more than the proper use of all the styles, in the right place and at the right time:

> The aim of Clarity is that the audience should understand what is said, whereas Grandeur is designed to impress them with what is said. Beauty is designed to give pleasure, Speed to avoid boredom, Ethos helps to win over the audience by allying them with the speaker's customs and character, and Verity persuades them he is speaking the truth. Finally Gravity . . . stirs up the audience, and they are carried away by the completeness of the performance, not only to accept what they have heard, but to act upon it.[4]

I should forewarn the reader about one matter. In his treatise Hermogenes often says that he will treat a particular topic in his discussion of Force. However, when he arrives at that ultimate point in the work he feels unable to do justice to the topic and says that he will discuss it in a separate treatise. At first he refers to the treatise as if it were already written, but then he reveals that that is not the case. We do not know whether he ever actually wrote it, but it is not extant. The essay "Practical Oratory," which closes this treatise, is essentially a brisk application of his basic criteria for Force to examples from authors whom he ranks as best and second-best among the most illustrious practitioners of deliberative, judicial, and panegyric oratorical styles.

Hermogenes claims in his preface to this work that he is describing pure types (*ideai*) of style in the abstract. In fact the term *idea* may indicate that his concept of an ideal form of style is derived from Platonic philosophy. But he also points out that the only orator who uses all these types as they should be used is Demosthenes, and his examples almost always come from that fourth-century B.C. politician, whom he usually refers to simply as "the orator." Thus in many ways the work is more than anything a description of Demosthenic style.[5] At the end of Book 2, however, when Hermogenes discusses Force in terms of the three types of oratory—the judicial, the epideictic (panegyric), and the deliberative—he also treats other individual writers in terms of the system that he has already outlined.

What was the source of this complex theory? It is unlikely that it was completely original with Hermogenes, although it is difficult to trace its development with certainty. Its ultimate source was probably the virtues of style—purity or correctness, clarity, propriety, and ornamentation—developed by Theophrastus at the end of the fourth century B.C. In the works of Dionysius of Halicarnassus, at the end of the first century B.C., we see that this list of stylistic virtues has been expanded.[6] (Dionysius, too, greatly admired the speeches of Demosthenes as the embodiment of all stylistic virtues.) A rhetorical treatise of the second century A.D., falsely attributed to Aelius Aristides, outlines twelve "ideas" of style. That work, which may have been written by Basilicus of Nicomedia,[7] was probably one of Hermogenes' sources. In any case it is quite clear that *On Types of Style* is the culmination of a tendency in Greek rhetorical criticism to refine more and more the concept of stylistic virtues that had been begun by Theophrastus.

Hermogenes' system soon replaced the concept of the three styles—the plain, the middle, and the grand—which had probably been developed during the Hellenistic period but which first appears in the *Rhetoric to Herennius* in the first century B.C. (see Appendix 1). In fact Hermogenes' work was destined to become the most influential treatise on style in later antiquity and Byzantine times, the standard textbook used in schools of rhetoric. In 1426 it was introduced into the West by George Trebizond, eventually translated into Latin by Gasparis Laurentius (1614), and again became a standard text, thus exerting as much influence on the Renaissance as it had in earlier times.[8]

I should say a word about the translation and about Hermogenes' own use of language. He is a brilliant critic of style whose own style is really quite atrocious. His language is often very tortuous, sometimes extremely compressed, sometimes excessively redundant. The work was probably written by a young man, possibly even a teenager, and it is filled with all the self-assurance, overstatement, and exuberance that one often associates with a high-school essay. In translating, though I have found it impossible to follow Hermogenes' Greek literally in every instance, I have tried to adhere to the text as closely as possible wherever that would not produce awkward English. Elsewhere I have taken the liberty of reordering his sentences and even, on occasion, of paraphrasing the text. Moreover, I have often explained technical terms with a bracketed paraphrase in the translation itself, and sometimes, for the sake of clarity, I have similarly expanded his comments somewhat, rather than referring the reader to the notes, which in my opinion unnecessarily interrupt the reading of the text. This work has no literary merit of its own. It is the content that is important, not the form; and that is why I have felt free to take more liberties with the text than I normally would have done.

I have relied on the Greek text by Hugo Rabe and have consulted the most important of the ancient commentaries on Hermogenes, that of Syrianus from the fifth century A.D., whose text was also established by Rabe. I have also consulted Gasparis Laurentius' Latin translation of 1614 and have been greatly helped by the English translation of some passages given in Donald Russell and Michael Winterbottom, *Ancient Literary Criticism*, 561–579.

Page numbers of Rabe's Greek edition are supplied in the margins of the present translation, and the numbers in my indices refer to them, so that readers can compare passages readily. Citations within the text are to Demosthenes unless otherwise noted. Occasionally Hermogenes repeats a quotation in the course of a discussion; in most instances, where reiterations follow fairly closely on the first mention, citation numbers have not been repeated. Rabe cross-references such passages in his apparatus; my Index of Passages Cited lists all occurrences of each.

Hermogenes'

On Types of Style

Book I

Introduction

1 I think that the types (*ideai*) of style are perhaps the most necessary 213
subject for the orator to understand, both what their characteristics are
and how they are produced.[1] This knowledge would be indispensable to
anyone who wanted to be able to evaluate the style of others, either of
the older writers or of those who have lived more recently, with reference to what is excellent and accurate, and what is not. And if someone
wished to be the craftsman of fine and noble speeches himself, speeches
such as the ancients produced, an acquaintance with this theory is also
indispensable, unless he is going to stray far from what is accurate.
Indeed imitation and emulation of the ancients that depend upon mere
experience and some irrational knack cannot, I think, produce what is
correct, even if a person has a lot of natural ability. Natural abilities,
without some training, dashing off without guidance at random, could 214
in fact go particularly badly. But with a knowledge and understanding
of this topic, when anyone wishes to emulate the ancients he would not
fail even if he has only moderate ability. Of course he will be most
successful if he also has natural talents, in which case he would produce
a much better speech. But if we do not have natural abilities, we must
try to achieve what can be learned and taught, since that is in our
control. Those with less natural ability could quickly overtake those
who are naturally talented, by means of practice and correct training.

Since, therefore, the study of the types is so important and so necessary to those who want to be good speakers and good critics (and even
more so to those who want to do both), you should not be amazed if we
should discover that this is a difficult topic and not such as to require
simple handling. Nothing good can be produced easily, and I should be
surprised if there were anything better for men, since we are logical
animals, than fine and noble *logoi* and every kind of them.

Before I proceed to the actual instruction concerning each of these
topics, I shall make one preliminary point. Our discussion will not be
concerned with the style peculiar to Plato or Demosthenes or any other 215
writer, although that will be discussed later. For now, we propose to

consider each type in itself, to show, for example, what Solemnity is and how it is produced, or what Asperity is or Simplicity, and likewise in respect to the other types. But since we need this study in order to appreciate individual authors, if we choose the author who uses a style that is especially varied and that really combines all the types, in discussing his style we shall have discussed them all. For if we demonstrate the individual features of such an author and the general character of his work, what its constituents are, and what sort of thing it is and why, we shall have given an accurate account of every type of style and we shall have demonstrated how they can be combined and how, as a result of these combinations, the style can be poetical or unpoetical, panegyrical, deliberative, forensic, or, in general, of any particular kind.

Now, the man who, more than anyone else, practiced this kind of oratory and was continuously diversifying his style is, in my opinion, Demosthenes. Therefore if we discuss him and what is found in his work, we shall in effect have discussed all the types of style. No one 216 should criticize my approach or my choice of Demosthenes until he has studied everything that I am going to say. I think that if one will pay close attention to what follows, he will find me worthy of admiration, especially for my clarity of arrangement, rather than criticism.

This is the main point in reference to Demosthenes: he had so mastered political oratory that he was always combining styles everywhere. When he gave a deliberative speech, for example, he did not separate it rigorously from a judicial speech or a panegyrical speech, but mixed the characteristics of all three in the same speech, regardless of what kind of oratory he was practicing. Anyone who studies his style carefully will easily recognize this. But it seems to me to be very difficult to discover exactly what elements he uses to create such a style, elements which, in combination with one another, produce panegyric and other kinds of oratory. It is no less difficult, indeed, for one who has discovered them to explain them clearly. Nor is there anyone, as far as I know, who has yet dealt with this topic with precision and clarity. Those who have undertaken it have discussed it in a confused and hesitating way, and their accounts are totally muddled. Moreover, even those who have seemed to make valid observations about the orator, because they have 217 studied his works in detail, at least to the best of their ability, say little or nothing about the general characteristics of his work. In other words they do not discuss types of style such as Solemnity or Simplicity. Consequently, although they might tell us something about Demosthenes and the individual aspects of his work that they discuss, they tell us nothing about style in general or the types of style, whether in meter, in poetry, or in prose.

Now, although it is difficult to perceive these types and to explain them clearly and to avoid the faults of our predecessors, nevertheless we must attempt to do so in the manner that we proposed earlier. If we can demonstrate accurately and specifically, in reference to the individual elements and basic principles of composition that make up the style of Demosthenes, how many there are and how they are produced and in what way they are combined to generate this effect or that, we shall have discussed all the various styles in general. As Demosthenes himself says, "This is a bold promise, and it will soon be put to the test, and whosoever wishes will be my judge" (4.15).

These are the elements that make up the style of Demosthenes taken as a whole: Clarity, Grandeur, Beauty, Rapidity, Character, Sincerity, and Force. I say "taken as a whole" because these are interwoven and interpenetrate one another, for that is the nature of Demosthenes' style. Of these types some exist separately and by themselves, others have subordinate types under them through which they are produced, and others share certain elements in common with other types. In general, to repeat what I have just said, some of the types are classes of other more general types, some share common elements with other types, although they are quite distinct from all the others, and some exist on their own quite independently of the others. Exactly what I mean by all this will become clearer as we proceed to discuss each type individually.

But first we must state the elements that are common to all speeches and without which no speech could exist, since once we have understood these we shall follow more easily when we discuss the subordinate types, mentioned earlier, out of which other types are produced.

Every speech has a thought or thoughts, an approach to the thought, and a style that is appropriate to these.[2] Likewise, style has its own peculiar properties: figures [of speech], clauses (*kōla*), word order, cadences, and rhythm.[3] Rhythm is produced by word order and pauses, since to arrange words in a certain way and to pause at certain times gives the speech a certain rhythm.

219   Since what I have said may not be clear, I shall clarify it with an example. Suppose you want to create Sweetness. The thoughts that are characteristic of Sweetness are those that are related to mythology and similar topics, which we shall discuss later in the section on Sweetness. The approaches [or modes of treating the subject matter] involve dealing with the topic as the principal theme and in a narrative fashion rather than treating it allusively or in some other indirect way. The style is that which depends much on adjectives and is subtle; if poetical, it must avoid elevation and natural diffuseness. All diction characteristic of Purity will also be appropriate. Figures of speech are permitted, but only those that involve straightforward grammar and no interruptions. The clauses should be short, a little longer than *kommata* or even equal to *kommata*. The arrangement of the words, because of the nature of the diction, should be relaxed but should not, on the other hand, be totally disjointed, since some of the pleasure derived from Sweetness is achieved through rhythm. The basic metrical unit employed should be dactylic ($^-$ $^\smile$ $^\smile$) or anapaestic ($^\smile$ $^\smile$ $^-$). (Anyone who discusses rhythm and word order should also treat syllables and letters, since rhythm is created from these, along with cadences, as will become clear later in our discussion. The cadences appropriate to Sweetness are rather

220   stately.) Rhythm results from word order and cadence, although it is separate from them, just as the shape of a house or of a ship is created when stones or pieces of wood are put together in a certain way with certain restrictions placed on the construction, although the shape of the house or of the ship is quite different from the manner of putting the building materials together and the limitations on that.[4]

All kinds of style, consequently, can be classified under the following headings, which denote those factors through which a particular style is produced: thought, approach, diction, figures, clauses, word order, cadence, and rhythm. I am sure that in spite of what has already been said there is need for some further clarification about these matters, but I do not agree with those who think that they can be clarified by means of examples. Of course I agree that examples should eventually be adduced, but I do not think that everything would be clear in this discussion if we brought forth some examples now. On the contrary, if we here produced examples of each of the factors mentioned above, the discussion would become very lengthy, and greater confusion might arise because of that. Moreover, it was not my object to discuss Sweetness at the moment, since we shall discuss that later in detail, but only to show through what factors each kind of style is produced in its pure state. Having been instructed concerning these things, we will be able, I hope, to follow the rest of the discussion more easily. To that I now return.

Thus every type of style is created out of the elements discussed above. But it is very difficult, nearly impossible in fact, to find among any of the ancients a style that is throughout composed of elements such as thought, approach, diction, etc., characteristic of only one kind of style; it is by the predominance of features belonging to one type that each acquires his particular quality. I exclude Demosthenes. Unlike others, he does not favor features that are characteristic of one particular type, although there is one subtype that he does use more often than the others. That is Abundance. (In the discussion of Grandeur and Abundance I shall discuss in detail why that is the case.) But as I was saying, he shows a preference only for a style that is a fraction or subclass of one type. Otherwise he uses each type when and where it should be used. He can scale down excessively elevated and brilliant thoughts by certain approaches or figures or by some other means.[5] Similarly, he can raise up and give vigor to thoughts that are trivial and of little importance. And in a similar way, by mixing each of the other types with features that are not appropriate or peculiar to it, he diversifies his style and thus makes everything fit together and creates a unity in which all the various types are interwoven. Thus from all the beauties of style, this one, the Demosthenic, the most beautiful, has been created.

Therefore, as I said before, strictly speaking, it is not possible to find accurately in any of the ancient orators a single style, because it is clearly a mistake to use only one and not to vary one's style. But each has a predominance of characteristics that are typical of one style or another, and that is what produces his own peculiar style. By "having a predominance of" I do not mean that he uses a greater number of those elements that create a particular type, such as approach, figures, word order, cadence, etc., although that may be so, but that he uses those elements that are most characteristic of each type. This is really what creates a particular type, and "having a predominance of" means "uses those elements that are most effective in creating each type." Sometimes,

221

222

if someone uses, even excessively, some of the factors that produce a particular style but does not employ those that are most characteristic of that style, he will fail to produce the effect at which he was aiming. We shall turn now to the effect that is produced by the various elements that make up the different styles.

First of all, and the most important, is the thought. Second comes the diction. Third in importance are figures of speech and fourth are figures of thought, which are the same as the approach. Figures of thought, however, hold the most important position in the type Force, where they are the most important of all the elements that produce that style, as will be shown later. We shall put word order and cadence last, although they are often more important than their ranking here would indicate, especially in poetry. For one of these factors without the other contributes little or nothing to the style of the speech, but together, especially in combination with rhythm, they can have a tremendous impact. Musicians, in fact, would probably argue that they are more important than the thought itself. They will say that rhythm in and of itself, even without any meaningful speech, is more effective than style. And suitable rhythms, they say, can please the soul more than any panegyrical speech, or cause it more pain than any rhetorical appeal to pity, or stir up our spirits more than any vehement and violent speech. They may provoke us about all these points, but we shall not quarrel with them. Put rhythm first or last in importance or in the middle, as you wish. I shall be content to show what rhythms are appropriate to each type of style and to what extent rhythm can be applied to prose without turning it into song. If rhythm is as important in prose style as it is in music, let it be put first in importance. If not, it will be put in the order of importance that seems suitable to me. My feeling is that rhythm does sometimes contribute a great deal to the production of one style rather than another, but not so much as the musicians say.

We have summarized briefly everything that has been said previously, and now we shall come to a discussion of the types themselves. We have already discussed (a) what the elements are that create the types of style, (b) what the effect of these is, (c) from what elements the style of Demosthenes is composed, and (d) why we think that it is necessary to choose this orator as our example. I also made the following point: it is not possible to find any of the types of style, such as Solemnity, used

continuously and elaborated in isolation from the other types in any of
the ancient orators—unless one calls an individual manner of speaking
a "type" and speaks, for example, of the "Demosthenic" or "Platonic"
type. Moreover, since it is not possible to understand or appreciate a
mixture, in reference to style or anything else, and it is certainly not
possible to create a mixture until we recognize the various elements out
of which the mixture was created (to understand gray, for example, we
must first understand black and white), we must ignore the style of
individual writers such as Plato, Demosthenes, and Xenophon and proceed to examine separately the most basic elements of style itself. One   225
who starts from this point can then easily go on to appreciate and describe individual authors, detecting their careful combinations, whether
he wants to study and emulate one of the ancients or someone more
recent.

Let us thus proceed to our subject and discuss the types from which
the style of Demosthenes is composed. By separating out the various
subtypes from which these are created and by observing how they are
woven together, we shall be able to define each of them accurately. The
types that are blended together in the style of Demosthenes are these:
Clarity, Grandeur, Beauty, Rapidity, Character, Sincerity, and Force.
We shall discuss all of these, but first we shall explain Clarity and the
subtypes that create it. You should not be surprised to find that some
types share certain characteristics with others. A certain thought or
subject matter, for example, or a certain type of diction might be characteristic of several types. The use of simple clauses with the noun in
the nominative case (*to tēs orthotētos schēma*), for example, such as in
the sentence "There is a certain Sannio, the man who trains tragic
choruses" (21.58), is characteristic both of Clarity and Simplicity. Such
a sentence is both clear and simple. This is true of other features of style
as well. Likewise Asperity and Florescence have thoughts that are common to both of them. Reproaches, for example, are usually delivered in
the rough style that we have called Asperity. But if they are delivered
[not in short, choppy clauses, but] in longer clauses with some amplification, they create Florescence, [which is a milder form of criticism].
Similarly Florescence shares certain characteristics with Brilliance. Each
type is different from the others although it might share similar features   226
with them, just as men are different from the other animals but in being

mortal they are similar to them, and we are different from the gods in that we are mortal but we are similar to them in that we are reasonable creatures. Likewise some of the types have characteristics that are common to other types.

But this is enough about preliminary matters. Now we must proceed to the discussion of Clarity, the opposite of which is obscurity (*asapheia*), and we have put it first since every speech needs to be clear. The elements out of which Clarity is produced are Purity and Distinctness.

Clarity (*Saphēneia*)

2 As I said, Purity and Distinctness create Clarity. Purity is produced by all the factors discussed above: thought, approach, diction, etc. Distinctness, on the other hand, is mainly a question of approach, although some of the other factors discussed above might also contribute to it.

First of all we must discuss Purity, the opposite of which in some ways, but not all, is Abundance, which we shall treat in the discussion of Grandeur and Dignity.

227 ## Purity (*Katharotēs*)

3 The thoughts that are characteristic of Purity are common, everyday thoughts that occur to everyone. They are clear, even without any explanation, and familiar to most people and are not at all recondite or abstruse. Examples are the sentence given earlier, "There is a certain Sannio, the man who trains tragic choruses" (21.58), or "The Thirty Tyrants are said to have borrowed money from the Spartans to be used against those who were in the Peiraeus" (20.11). We should look at these thoughts by themselves, and not at the reasons for their use, because if we do that, we shall suspect that they have other qualities and are not really "pure," although they are in fact perfectly pure if they are considered on their own. Pure thoughts are thus very often used to introduce a topic, such as when Demosthenes begins two speeches with the sentences "Spoudias and I have wives who are sisters" (41.1) or

"Men of Athens, I am a sharer of this loan" (56.1). In general there are many examples of these kinds of thoughts in Demosthenes' private speeches and quite a few even in the public speeches.

There is really only one approach that is appropriate to this type. A speech is especially pure and clear when someone narrates a simple fact and begins with the fact itself and does not add anything that is extraneous to the topic. The speaker will not amplify his theme, for example, by discussing the genus of which what he is narrating is only a species, or by discussing the whole of which it is only a part. He will not treat what is indefinite about his topic or what is unclear, or bring in the judgment of judges, or talk about the quality of the act that he is narrating or compare it with other events, or anything like that. All those approaches are characteristic of Abundance, which is the opposite of Purity. One can also create Abundance by discussing aspects of 228 an action that are related to it, [but not really necessary to understanding what took place,] such as place, time, actor, manner, or cause. But a speech that is pure must completely overlook these aspects of an action in its approach, or at least it must not relate them until the bare facts of the situation have been set forth. Even someone who discusses these [basically extraneous] matters, or some of them, can make his speech appear to be pure by employing other aspects of style that create Purity, such as figures and diction, and this is a sort of approach that is characteristic of Purity. Such a speaker will give the impression of speaking "purely," but that will not really be the case. And in fact he will be amplifying the topic.

It is easy to see this approach in the works of Demosthenes. When he says, for example, "Having been insulted, gentlemen of Athens, and having suffered such things at the hands of Conon here" and so on (54.1), he has put everything in a pure way for the sake of the introduction of the subject, and the examples cited earlier illustrate the same technique. He has started with the bare facts of the case, and these passages consequently have an appearance of Purity and ordinary common speech. In each case what is said next amplifies the topic, although it is not really noticeable since the introduction has been straightforward. Thus it is clear from these examples that sometimes speeches can appear to be pure when they are not so in fact.

It is characteristic of the approach that is most typical of Purity to use narration and not to introduce the facts of the case in any other way. For narration is an approach, not a figure, as some think. You could use 229 many figures in your narration, nominative cases and oblique cases, subdivisions and divisions. Generally, in fact, a narration is created out of many figures, and things that are figures themselves are not usually created out of other figures. Narration must thus be considered an approach. In any case, whether it is an approach or a figure, one must realize that narration is useful in creating Purity. These, then, are the topics and approaches that are characteristic of this type of style.

The diction that is appropriate to Purity is everyday language that everyone uses, not that which is abstruse or harsh-sounding. When Homer says, for example, "He climbed the rough track" (*Od.* 14.1), the word "track" sounds unusual here as does the phrase in Demosthenes, "ate it right up [the man's nose]" (25.62). In fact there are other examples of this in Demosthenes: "hamstrung" (3.31), "having sold himself" (19.13), and "mutilating and mugging and ravaging Greece" (9.22). These expressions and expressions like them are vivid and give the style a certain Grandeur, but they are not pure. That is why with many of these expressions there is a need for clarification. When Demosthenes says "hamstrung," for example, he then explains what he means by adding "since you have been stripped of your money and your allies," and this makes the thought clearer. (The style of Isocrates, by the way, is generally very pure.)

The figure that is most characteristic of Purity is the use of a straightforward construction with the noun in the nominative case (*orthotēs*), as Demosthenes does when he says, "For I, gentlemen of Athens, fell out with a worthless and quarrelsome man" (24.6). As I was saying before, it is necessary to consider this statement on its own and to see whether it is pure, regardless of what is said after it. For what is said 230 next does not allow the style to remain pure. That is the case also with the examples mentioned earlier about Sannio and the wives who were sisters. I can prove that the use of straightforward sentences with the subject in the nominative case is most characteristic of Purity. If you use the oblique cases, even though you are narrating facts, you always amplify the speech. The oblique cases, since their use involves subordinate clauses, introduce other, unnecessary thoughts. And just as the use of simple clauses with the subject in the nominative case is the opposite of complex sentences where the subject of an action is often in an oblique case, so Abundance, taken as a whole, is the opposite of Purity, taken as a whole.

What I mean will be clear from the following example. If you say "Candaules was" and "Croesus was," using a straightforward sentence with the subject in the nominative case, you make the sentence pure and clear. If you use subordination[6] and say "When Croesus was" or "Since Candaules was," the style is no longer pure and clear. There is at the outset some confusion, since it is necessary that some other thought follow, and the lengthy expression produces a certain lack of Clarity. If Herodotus, for example (1.7), had said, "Since Croesus was a Lydian by birth, and since he was the son of Alyattes, and since he ruled those nations on this side of the Halys River," the point that he really wanted to make would have been kept in suspense; [and this does not make for Clarity]. And it would be even less clear if the subordination at the beginning of the sentence were prolonged. But Herodotus uses short clauses that are marked off from one another by brief pauses: "Croesus was a Lydian by birth, and he was the son of Alyattes, and he ruled those nations." In general, therefore, any means of expression that does not amplify the thought makes the style pure. 231

Let me take another example. In the speech *Against Meidias* (13) Demosthenes says, "For when I came forward and volunteered to serve as chorus master, [when the assembly at which the archon assigned the flute-players was meeting . . . and when there were arguments and disputes, since the tribe of Pandionis for two years had not appointed one, you, gentlemen of Athens, welcomed my offer]." This sentence is amplified, both in thought and by figures, [by reason of the many thoughts that are expressed in it and because Demosthenes here uses three levels of subordination]. If, however, you wanted to retain the details of the incident, which is characteristic of Abundance, but to nar-rate them in a way that is characteristic of Purity, you would say: "For two years the tribe of Pandionis had not appointed a chorus master. The assembly was meeting. The archon was assigning the flute-players. There were arguments and disputes. I came forward and offered my services." And if someone should express all his thoughts in such a way he would make his speech clearer, although it would have no Grandeur or power so far as the diction and its features are concerned.

You should not be surprised if we have mentioned Abundance as if you knew what it was in spite of the fact that we have not really discussed it. In a stylistic discussion of this sort that is the only way to proceed; [We would have had to use comparisons and contrasts] even if we had begun our discussion with another style other than Clarity. For almost all the types of style can best be described by looking at them in relation to other types. Sometimes this can best be done by contrast, as here, when we said that those means of expression are pure that are the opposite of those that create Abundance. Sometimes the point can be made more clearly by means of comparison. This was our approach at the beginning of the present discussion when we stated that Clarity is produced by Distinctness and Purity, although we had not yet defined clearly what these were. But [just as we eventually explained Purity, and shall soon explain Distinctness,] so eventually we shall also discuss 232 Abundance. Now we must return to our discussion. [First, though, I want to make a final point about expression.] Unnatural word order or twisted and contorted sentences are also detrimental to Purity, and these, like Abundance, must also be avoided to be clear.

We now turn to a discussion of the kinds of clauses that are most characteristic of Purity. It is clear from what has already been said that these should be short, like *kommata*, and that they should express complete thoughts in themselves. Long clauses and periodic sentences are inappropriate in a pure style.

The structure of a pure sentence must first of all be straightforward and consist of only one clause, and there should be little concern about avoiding hiatus. The avoidance of hiatus is more typical of an elaborate style than of one that is straightforward and pure. The rhythm should be rather prosaic and conversational and should use metrical configurations such as iambs ($\smile\,-$) and trochees ($-\,\smile$) [into which conversation naturally falls], as Demosthenes does in the following sentence (24.6): *egō gar, ō Athēnaioi, prosekrousa anthrōpōi ponērōi*. It is not necessary to demand precision here, nor is it possible. It is enough for the feet at the beginning of the sentence to consist of iambs and trochees and for the rest of the sentence to contain more iambs and trochees than dactyls ($-\,\smile\,\smile$), anapests ($\smile\,\smile\,-$), and other less conversational meters. Indeed it is appropriate that other meters be mixed with the 233 iambs and the trochees so that the style does not become completely metrical. In other words the sentence should have some natural rhythm but it should not be regularly metrical like poetry. Prose rhythm, which is created by word order and cadence, should be metrical to some extent but not overly so. The meter that is appropriate will be determined by the kind of style that is being used. Here, for example, as we have said, iambs and trochees are most suitable for Purity. However, to give an example of what I was saying before, in the line *hoútos* | *ástrat-* | *eĭ-* | *as hĕ-* | *álō* | *kaī kĕ-* | *chrḗtaī* | *symphŏ-* | *raī* (21.58) there is a brief interruption of the regular metrical pattern in the word *astrateias* since the last syllable is long where one would expect a short syllable. In fact, if you wanted to excuse this, you could call it a pure trochaic tetrameter catalectic, which normally consists of four pairs of trochees, although a spondee (⁻ ⁻) can be substituted for a trochee. But I have said enough about the word order that is appropriate to Purity.

And it should be clear from what I have already said that the cadences should be similar to the metrical configurations produced by the order of the words. In other words, if iambs and trochees have predominated in the rest of the sentence, the final cadence should also be iambic or trochaic so that the overall rhythm of the sentence, which is produced by word order and cadences, will be primarily iambic or trochaic. That means that the prose will be metrical in nature but not strictly metrical like poetry. [So the cadences used in Purity should be iambic or trochaic.] 234

All these factors—the word order, insofar as it falls into regular metrical patterns; the cadences; and the rhythm of the entire sentence, which results from word order and cadence—are difficult to grasp and have consequently been explained by us in great detail. They do not, however, contribute very much to Purity of style, although they do contribute something. This is the case with most, if not all, types of style as well, as I said earlier when I mentioned musicians and argued that metrical considerations are less important in producing a particular style than other factors. It is really the subject matter, and the diction, and the approaches, and the types of clauses and figures used, that create one style or another, although rhythmical considerations do have some effect. In some of the types, in fact, rhythm is very important, especially in Beauty and any sort of well-wrought style, as will be very clear when we discuss Beauty. Such considerations are obviously also extremely important in poetry, but that does not concern us here and it is quite evident to everyone. Therefore let this discussion concerning Purity come to a close.

235 Distinctness (*Eukrineia*)

4 Distinctness possesses some characteristics that naturally produce Clarity, but in general it is the ally of Purity in attaining the aim of that type of style. The goal of Purity is to make the speech clear, and Distinctness sets the speech back on the right course and makes it clear what the speaker is doing if there is any unavoidable obscurity in it, as often happens in public speaking. Distinctness is primarily concerned with the approach of the speech. It is the function of Distinctness to determine what aspects of the case the judges should consider first and what they should consider second and to make that clear to them. When Demosthenes, for example, says in the speech *On the False Embassy* (4), outlining how he will handle the argument, "What should be included in the account that an ambassador makes to the city of his embassy? He should discuss first of all what reports he made, and secondly what advice he gave, and thirdly what instructions you gave to him," he brings considerable Clarity to his presentation, especially since in the speech he does not intend to deal with the facts of the case in chronological order but very forcefully deals with later events first (although we cannot consider here why that is a forceful approach). To treat events out of their normal chronological sequence often makes a speech clearer and also more forceful. That is what Demosthenes does in the speech *Against Aristocrates* (8). But he forewarns the audience that he will take that approach: "First of all I must explain why you hold the Chersonese safely." Then he explains that it [the reason] is the quarrel among the 236 Thracians. For what he wanted to demonstrate would have been unclear if he had attacked Charidemus first on the grounds that he was furthering the power of Cersobleptes and then said, "Why then do you hold the Chersonese safely?"[7] But as it is, he has established at the very outset, in the proemium to the speech, before discussing Charidemus and Cersobleptes, that he is concerned about how the Athenians can safely hold the Chersonese and will not through deception be stripped of it again. And having made it clear at the outset that it is important for the Athenians to encourage dissension among the Thracians if they want to maintain their holdings in the Chersonese, he has made the speech distinct and clear. Whether this approach is also forceful is another question.

As I was saying, the approach is primarily responsible for making a speech distinct, although other factors also can create the same effect. Thoughts, for example, that give appropriate background material make the speech distinct, such as the following that one finds in Demosthenes (18.17): "It is necessary, men of Athens, and fitting as well, to remind you what the situation was like in those times so that you might consider how it relates, in all its details, to the present crisis." Thoughts that delineate clearly what is going to be said and in what order also create Distinctness, as Demosthenes does in the following passage (23.18): "I have undertaken to demonstrate to you three things, first that the decree is illegal, second that it is not in the city's best interests, and third that 237 Charidemus is not worthy to obtain what you have proposed, and it is perhaps just that you choose what point I will argue first." Then he says, "If you want to consider the illegality of the decree first, I will discuss that now." I have often asserted that what I have said should not be criticized if the example that I have given involves something in addition to Distinctness. The passage cited above is clever and forceful as well as being distinct, but this is not the place to discuss that.

Moreover, "completions" (sympléroseis), thoughts and approaches that signal that one train of thought is being brought to a close and that another is being introduced, also make the speech distinct, especially when the speaker makes clear the nature of the new thought, as Demosthenes does in the following passage (18.136): "One of this hothead's political acts was such as I have described. Let me remind you of another." Then he begins this section of the speech, "When Philip sent Pytho of Byzantium," etc. He uses the same approach when he says (20.41), "It is necessary to consider not only how Leucon may not be treated unjustly, but also whether any other has done you a service," etc. There are many examples of this, but these illustrate what thoughts are characteristic of Distinctness.

In addition to the approaches already discussed it is also characteristic of Distinctness to follow in the speech the natural order of events and

238 arguments, putting first things first and second things second, as Isocrates does so often. This is not particularly forceful and is not characteristic of Demosthenes. That is why he uses techniques that make his approach clear, as we showed a little earlier, although sometimes it is more forceful to adhere to the natural order of things. But we will discuss that more precisely in our treatment of the approach that is characteristic of Force.

Moreover, if one follows the natural order of topics, to put the counterproposition (*antithesis*) before its refutation (*lysis*) creates Distinctness. Isocrates almost always does this, although Demosthenes is inconsistent in this respect. The latter arranges his material in such a way that it will be most beneficial to his own point of view, sometimes putting the counterproposition first and sometimes last and sometimes in the middle. At times, in other words, he refutes the arguments of his opponent before he offers his own proposals. At other times he introduces his own proposal first, and sometimes he puts his own proposal in the middle of the refutation of the arguments of his opponent. We will discuss more precisely how proposals should be introduced in the section on the approach that is most characteristic of Force. These, however, are the approaches that make for Distinctness. And the style that creates Distinctness is the same as that which is characteristic of Purity.

The figures that are characteristic of Distinctness include, first of all, definition by means of enumerating the components that make up a group (*to kat' athroisin hōrismenon*), such as "Here he said two things, this and that." Thus the hearer does not expect more than two things and foresees what is going to be said second. And so, by accumulating various entities that make up a group, the speaker makes it clear beforehand what he will say. Similarly, dividing a whole into its parts (*merismos*) and enumerating its characteristics (*aparithmēsis*) create Distinctness.

239 The introduction of new thoughts generally amplifies and expands a speech, but if the speaker shows to his audience at the outset of his argument what new thought will follow he has made his whole approach clear from the beginning. If he says, "I will treat this first," he notifies the audience that he will say something else second. Demosthenes does this at the beginning of the speech *On the Chersonese* when he says, "On the one hand (*men*), public speakers ought," and this causes the audience to expect that he will answer the anticipatory conjunction. These are some of the approaches that are characteristic of Distinctness.

A speech also becomes distinct whenever the speaker asks himself a question and then replies after a brief pause. Demosthenes often does this by saying something like "Why do I say this?" or "How then is this true?" or "Why is this so?" He uses many such devices in the speech *Against Aristocrates*, since he is examining an illegal procedure, a topic that demands a great deal of Clarity. Repetitions (*epanalēpseis*) also are especially useful when the orator wants to create Distinctness and Clarity. When you introduce a thought in such a way that another thought will logically follow, but then are forced to deal with other matters before coming to the thought that has already been promised, you must repeat what you have said earlier, so that your organization will not seem to be confused and unclear. Demosthenes often does this. In the *Second Olynthiac*, for example, he says: "I do not choose to discuss Philip's strength and by such arguments to urge you to do what is necessary. Why?" (3). Then he gives his reasons. Although he then says many things that support his basic point of view, he does not in- 240 troduce immediately the thought that seems to follow naturally from what had been said before, namely "But there are other matters that I will discuss" (4). This procedure could have made the speech unclear. Therefore he repeats, in effect, what he had said earlier, "I will pass over these topics" (4), before introducing the matters that he will discuss. That has made the speech distinct and clear. In the speech *On the False Embassy*, moreover, he says: "Why then do I say this? My first and most important reason, gentlemen of Athens, is so that none of you should be amazed when you hear me relating certain episodes" (25). Then after interjecting many details and completing his argument on this point, he repeats what he had said earlier so that the argument will be clear: "This was the first and most important reason for narrating these facts. And what was the second, which is no less important than the first?" (27). There are, in fact, many examples of this technique in Demosthenes. But this is enough discussion of the figures that create Distinctness. The clauses, the arrangement of the words, the cadences, and the rhythms that produce Distinctness are the same as those that are characteristic of Purity.

Let this discussion suffice concerning Clarity. One must realize (I feel quite sure of this) that a speech will not be clear if it does not exemplify the characteristics that produce Purity or Distinctness, or at least some of them. The opposite of Distinctness is confusion, which happens whenever a speaker deals with a topic verbosely and at great length but does not employ those techniques that create Distinctness. That is a defect. But lack of Clarity in and of itself is not always a fault, since indirect expressions (*emphaseis*), such as "And there were those supporting the proposal for some reason—but I will pass over that" (18.21), and "figured problems" do not narrate facts clearly, although we cannot say that they have been introduced in a faulty way or make a speech defective.[8] But that brings up the question of Grandeur, which we shall treat in the next section. Clarity needs a certain amount of Grandeur and majesty (*onkos*), since insignificance and vulgarity are not far away from extreme Clarity, and Grandeur is the counter to that.

Dignity (*Axiōma*) and Grandeur (*Megethos*)

5 It is only natural to discuss Grandeur after the discussion of Clarity, for it is necessary to interject Grandeur and a certain amount of majesty and dignity into a clear passage. This is because the very clear can seem trite and commonplace, which is the opposite of Grandeur. I am sure that Demosthenes recognized this. He knew that the style of a political speech must be very clear and, consequently, consistently uses those elements that produce Clarity. But since he also realized that because of this there was a danger that his style might degenerate into the commonplace, he mixed in elements that produce Grandeur, especially Abundance. We shall discuss why he especially uses Abundance in the discussion of that topic. But now, to keep our analysis clear, we must discuss Grandeur and those types that produce Grandeur, one of which is Abundance.

The types that produce Grandeur and majesty and dignity are the following: Solemnity, Abundance, Asperity, Brilliance, Florescence, and Vehemence, which does not differ much from Asperity, as will be clear when we discuss it. Of these styles Solemnity and Abundance exist on their own, but all the others are connected (and also not connected) in some way with other types, that is, they share some characteristics with other styles but are quite distinct from them in other ways. I shall discuss Solemnity now and the other styles later. Although Abundance can also exist on its own, as I said before, I shall postpone discussion of it since Demosthenes uses it often and we cannot understand why he is so fond of it to give majesty and "bulk" to a speech until we have learned something about Asperity, Brilliance, Florescence, and Vehemence. First, then, we shall discuss Solemnity, the opposite of which, I suppose, is Simplicity, which we shall discuss in the section on Character.

Solemnity (*Semnotēs*)

6 Solemn thoughts are those concerning the gods, at least when they are spoken of as gods. Things like "The son of Cronos grasped his wife in his arms" (Homer *Il*. 14.346) are not expressed speaking of the gods   243 as gods, since they seem to me to be far from solemn and as far as the thought is concerned are charming and sweet rather than solemn. They are poetical expressions of human feelings, and generally, I think, the main aim of poetry is pleasure. But the following have been said, I think, of gods as gods: "He was good, and a good being does not feel envy of anything" or "God wanted all things to be good and nothing to be bad as far as was in his power" or "God took everything that was visible, when it was not at rest but moving in disharmony and disorder." In general you could find many such thoughts in Plato, and these, in fact, come from the *Timaeus* (29e, 30a, 30a). But there are not many examples in the orators, since even Hyperides' *Deliacus* is really poetical and mythical rather than oratorical; why that is so, I do not need to explain here.[9]

You could find in Demosthenes, however, and even some of the other orators, thoughts that comprise a second or third order of Solemnity. The first order, as I have said, are those thoughts that discuss the gods as gods. The second order of solemn thoughts are those that discuss truly divine things, such as inquiries into the nature of the seasons and how and why they are caused, and circular motion, and the nature of the universe, or inquiries into how the movements of the earth and of the sea are caused or how thunderbolts are produced. All such thoughts   244 comprise the second order of Solemnity. If these matters are treated only in respect to their causes they can make the speech solemn but not appropriate for a practicing politician. How appropriate would it be for a statesman to say "the sun, since it is driven away during the winter season" and the comments that follow this in Herodotus (2.24)?[10] Or this passage from Plato (*Tim.* 58a): "The path of the universe, being circular and encompassing all things, binds them together from every direction and allows no place to be left empty. Wherefore fire has pervaded everything, then air, since it is the second lightest element, and then so on with the other things," etc.? And how would it be appropriate in practical oratory to inquire how earthquakes are produced and whether it is by the overflowing or recession of water or how thunderbolts are generated or other such matters? As I was saying, if these topics are handled thus, they make the speech solemn, but they do not give it any practical value as oratory. Thus these comprise the second class of thoughts that are characteristic of Solemnity.

If, however, one deals with these topics in a descriptive passage (*ekphrasis*) that depicts the events themselves, but does not try to explain their causes, this makes the speech solemn and can also give it value as practical oratory. This is what Aristides does when he attacks Callixenus, who was advising the Athenians not to give proper burial to the ten generals who had been condemned by a single vote.[11] In order to defend them Aelius Aristides composes an *ekphrasis* on the storm: "It was a sudden storm, Callixenus, a sudden storm, that cannot be de-

245   scribed and that could not be resisted, that prevented them from saving the men. Almost as soon as the battle had begun, the sea began to swell and a strong wind blowing from the Hellespont swooped down on them."

The third order of thoughts that produce Solemnity are those dealing with matters that are by nature divine but are often seen in human affairs, such as the immortality of the soul or justice or moderation or other such concepts, or inquiries into life in general or what is law or what is nature or other such questions. The following are examples from Demosthenes: "Law is an invention and a gift of the gods," etc. (25.16) or "The law is our common possession and well ordered and the same for all, whereas nature is without order and peculiar to each individual man" (25.15) or "Death is the end of life for all men" (18.97) or "All the life of men is governed by nature and by laws" (25.15). In a word, whatever is discussed generally and universally, especially if the speaker keeps the discussion general throughout, produces thoughts that are in some way solemn. But if you add some specific detail, the effect is not the same. That is what happens in Demosthenes' speech *On the Crown* when he says, "An informer is a bad thing, gentlemen of Athens, always a bad thing and everywhere malicious and carping," and then adds, "but this little man is also a rogue by nature" (242). Here adding a specific comment has changed the effect. By combining the general and the particular you create a style that is typical of practical oratory and 246 one that is abundant, but it is not necessarily solemn.

The fourth order of thoughts that produce Solemnity are those that deal with entirely human affairs, but those that are great and glorious, such as the battle at Marathon or Plateia or the sea battle at Salamis or cutting a canal through Mount Athos or bridging the Hellespont. And if you add an element of fable, as Herodotus does in the story of Iacchus [12] and elsewhere, the passage is solemn and charming as well. But that is another discussion. Here we end the one concerning thoughts that produce Solemnity.

The approaches that are characteristic of Solemnity are direct statements made without hesitation. For when we aim to produce consistent Solemnity, we must speak with dignity, and as one who is perfectly sure of what he says and does not hesitate. The thought "whether they were heroes or gods" is solemn as far as the content is concerned, but the expression of hesitation makes it more characteristic of practical oratory, which aims at persuasion. Allegorical approaches, if they are maintained, also produce a solemn style, as Plato does in the *Phaedrus* when he says, "Zeus, the great leader in heaven, rides his winged chariot," etc. (246e). I should add, however, that this happens only when someone decides to create an allegory out of elements that are not trite and commonplace. Such allegories do not create Solemnity but introduce a different sort of thought, often a vulgar one. Thirdly, to hint at something that would be a solemn thought, as is done in initiation ceremonies in mystery religions, is also an appropriate approach for Solemnity. If it seems that we ourselves know something that we cannot reveal clearly, 247 we thereby create a certain amount of Grandeur and Solemnity as far as the thought is concerned, as Plato does when he says in the *Timaeus* "truly being" or "He was a good man" (28c, 28d) and other such things. And in one passage Plato has extended this approach: "To discover this is a difficult matter and to reveal it to all once it has been discovered is impossible" (*Tim.* 28c). Such approaches are useful in augmenting the

Solemnity of the passage when the writer is dealing with thoughts that are by nature solemn. In more practical speeches, however, hints of Solemnity do not have the same effect. So much for the approaches and thoughts that are characteristic of Solemnity.

The diction that is appropriate for Solemnity consists of broad sounds that make us open our mouth wide when we pronounce them. We are thus forced by the nature of the words themselves to speak broadly, which some speakers do anyway. There are other possibilities, but long *a*'s and *o*'s especially produce this effect. That is why, according to Plato (*Phdr.* 244d), some people call *oiōnistikē* (augury) *ōōnistikē*, to make it sound more solemn by adding an extra long *o*. The same is true with long *a*. Theocritus (15.88), for example, depicts a man who is angry with women who, because they speak Doric, use lots of broad *a*'s in 248 their speech. Long *a*'s and *o*'s elevate and broaden speech especially if they occur in the final syllables of the words, as in Plato when he says, *ho men dē megas hēgemōn en ouranō Zeus*, "Zeus, the great leader in heaven" (*Phdr.* 246e).

Secondly, words that contain a short *o* and end in a long syllable, such as *Orontēs*, produce Solemnity, as do those that have a lot of long vowels and diphthongs and those that end in these, except for the diphthong *ei*. If long *i* is often used, it does not make the style solemn, since it contracts the mouth and makes us part our lips with our teeth closed rather than opening our mouth up.

Moreover, metaphorical expressions are solemn and grandiose, but one must be careful in using them. Used moderately they do make the speech solemn. If one says, for example, "projecting good hopes" (18.97) instead of "hoping for good things," that is appropriate. As you see, "projecting" is such a modest metaphor that it is not even noticed. Moderate metaphors or tropes are like that. But if a strong metaphor is used, the style becomes harsh, as happens in the expression "the cities were sick" (18.45). It needs explanation. When Demosthenes adds, "For those who managed the state were taking bribes," etc., he is simply explaining what he meant by "were sick." Very strong metaphors make a speech even harsher, as Demosthenes does when he says "they were hamstrung" (13.31) or "he sold himself" (19.16) or "he mugged Greece" (9.22). To use even bolder metaphors makes a speech coarse and vulgar. You could 249 not find any examples of this in Demosthenes, for there are none. In the works of pretentious sophists you would find very many indeed. They call vultures, whose attentions they themselves deserve, "living tombs" [13] and use other such frigid images. Tragedies, which contain many examples of such language, and poets, like Pindar, who use a tragic style have been their downfall. Perhaps we could defend the tragedians and Pindar when they use language in this way, although we must postpone this discussion since it is not appropriate here. But I find no excuse for those who use such crudities in practical oratory.

Fourthly, substantival words and nouns themselves make diction solemn. By "substantival words" I mean verbal forms that are used as nouns and participles and pronouns and other such forms. In fact, in a solemn style you should use as few verbs as possible. Thucydides, for example, consistently does this, but he has made it most obvious in his description of the Corcyraean revolution (3.82). There, except for the verb "was considered," all the other words are nouns or substantival forms, as in this passage and what follows it: "For irrational boldness was considered loyal heroism, and cautious delay a remarkable lack of courage, and moderation an excuse for cowardice." (Whether there is also an element of harshness or Asperity in this passage is none of my concern here.) And a phrase of Demosthenes, which he comments upon himself, is like this. He says, "He declared that words do not strengthen associations." Then he comments, "And this is an impressive way of describing the situation" (18.35). So much, then, for the diction that is appropriate to a solemn style.

The figures that produce Solemnity are the same as those that produce Purity, that is, simple, direct statements and the like. Moreover, added value judgments (*epikriseis*), whether they are thoughts or figures, are solemn: "To grant them by words what honor remains is enjoined by law, and is right" (Plato *Menex.* 236d) or "since they made a right and noble decision" (18.97). All such sentences are dignified and solemn. However, judgments that are expressed with some hesitation reveal Character, but they are not solemn. Demosthenes does this when he says, "Although I do not like abuse, I am, it seems, compelled to state the necessary facts" (18.126). In fact any hesitation generally makes the speech more expressive of Character. But anyone who intends to give some Grandeur and Solemnity to his speech must speak dogmatically: "Philip had no way of ending or escaping from the war with us" (18.145).

250

But if you say, "I do not think that Philip had any way," you reveal your own Character. On the other hand, to attribute to your own opinion [without hesitation or doubt] something of what you are about to say can produce Grandeur and Solemnity. If you say "I want to say this" or, as Thucydides says (1.9), "Agamemnon seems to me to have been pre-eminent among those who were in power at that time," that is solemn.

Direct addresses (*apostrophai*) and parentheses (*hypostrophai*) are not conducive to Solemnity or Purity. In fact they reduce and destroy the Solemnity or Purity of a passage by breaking it up with interruptions and by upsetting the free flow of the passage and by making it more conversational and typical of practical oratory. For example, if we put the phrase "whether they live in a large or a small city" in the middle of the sentence "The life of all men is governed by nature and by laws" (25.15), you would not get the same effect as you would if you did not interrupt the sentence with a parenthesis. To say "The life of all men, whether they live in a large or a small city, is governed by nature and by laws," is vigorous and rapid, while it is also typical of practical oratory and solemn. The sentence without the parenthesis is purely solemn, without the mixture of any other characteristic. Thus if our speech is going to remain solemn throughout, we must not interrupt it. If not, other measures must be taken.

The clauses (*kōla*) that are typical of Solemnity are the same as those that produce Purity, that is, short clauses that read like aphorisms: "Every soul is immortal, for what always moves is immortal" (Plato *Phdr.* 245c) or "Law is the invention and gift of the gods, and the judgment of wise men," etc. (25.16). Somewhat longer clauses, however, might sometimes have to be used in a solemn passage.

In arranging the words in the sentence to produce a solemn effect one should not be overly concerned about sounds that clash or hiatus and should aim at rhythms that are dactylic ($^-$ $^\smile$ $^\smile$) and anapaestic ($^\smile$ $^\smile$ $^-$) and paeonic ($^-$ $^\smile$ $^\smile$ $^\smile$ or $^\smile$ $^\smile$ $^\smile$ $^-$) and sometimes iambic ($^\smile$ $^-$) and often spondaic ($^-$ $^-$). Measures containing three longs and a short, called an epitrite, are also appropriate, but trochees ($^-$ $^\smile$) and ionics ($^-$ $^-$ $^\smile$ $^\smile$ or $^\smile$ $^\smile$ $^-$ $^-$) are not. The writer who corrupted the following verse from Homer made this clear:

$$\bar{sei\bar{o}n} \mid \bar{P\bar{e}lia}\breve{\text{-}} \mid \bar{da}\ \breve{meli}\breve{\text{-}} \mid \bar{en}\ \breve{kata} \mid \bar{dexion} \mid \bar{\bar{o}mon.}$$

(*Il.* 20.133)

By changing the words around you transpose the meter from dactylic to the ionic and the trochaic, which is related to the ionic, having only one short and one long where the ionic has two:

seiōn melĭ- | ēn Pēliă- | da | dexĭ- | on kăt'| ōmŏn.

Here there are two ionic pairs and then the so-called ithyphallic meter, which is composed of three trochees. Because of this rearrangement the whole rhythm has been broken down and forced into a pattern that is just the opposite of the dactylic, and other measures that are characteristic of Solemnity. You can see the same thing happen in many other verses. If you change the order of the words and, consequently, the rhythm, you produce a very different effect. For example, if you changed the order of the words in the following verses:

hōs hō | prosth' hĭp- | pōn kaī | dīphroū | keitŏ tă- | nystheĭs,
bebrȳ- | chōs, konĭ- | os dē- | dragmenŏs | haimatŏ- | essēs

(*Il.* 13.392–393)

you would produce the following mixed trochaic verses:[14]

hōs hō | prosth' hĭp- | pōn ĕ- | keitŏ | kai dī- | phroū tă- | nystheĭs,
haimă- | toēs- | sēs kō- | nios | dē- | dragmē- | nŏs, bĕ- | brychōs.

Likewise, in the following two passages, if the words were changed you could produce a trochaic tetrameter [measures of four double feet]:

253

hoi mĕn ĕp'akraisi pȳrais nekyĕs ĕkeintŏ
gēs epi xenēs orphanan aian prolipontĕs
hēbĕn t'erateinēn kai kalon hēliou prosōpon.

(anon)[15]

all'echŏn | hōs tĕ tăl- | lanta gȳ-| nē cher- | nētis ă- | lēthēs
hē tĕ | stathmōn ĕ-| chousă kai | eirion | amphis ă- | nelkei
isa- | zous', hina | paisin ă- | eikeă | misthon ă- | roitŏ.

(*Il.* 12.433–435)

The comments that we made concerning the cadences, or *clausulae*, that are typical of Purity, apply to the solemn style as well. It is necessary that the sentence come to a halt on one of those feet that are appropriate to Solemnity. This final foot must not be lacking a syllable at the end, what we call a catalectic foot, so that a dactyl, for example, might not become a trochee and the rhythm would be broken and become unsteady. The rhythm would be most firm if the sentence ended with a noun or some substantival form of at least three syllables, as Demosthenes does when he ends a sentence with the phrase *eis toutoni*

254 *ton agōna*, "to this case" (18.1). Also there could be more long syllables at the end of the sentence so that the metrical basis of the cadence becomes the double spondee or any epitrite except the fourth, which has the short syllable at the end. This is what Demosthenes does in the following sentence: *hapas ho tōn anthrōpōn bios phusei kai nomois dioikeĩtaĩ*, "All human life is controlled by nature and laws" (25.15). The rhythm is particularly solemn if the cadence has, either at the end or near the end, some broad sound that forces us to open our mouth wide when we pronounce it, as I said before in the discussion of the diction that is characteristic of Solemnity.

From this discussion the nature of rhythm should be clear. One must realize, however, that even if the rhythm of an entire speech has been based on epitrites, dactyls, and other feet, such as spondees, that are appropriate in a solemn style, but the cadences do not contain these metrical configurations (so that the beginning of the next sentence may maintain them), the rhythms are not solemn. This is true of every type of style. If a speech generally uses rhythms of a certain kind, which tend to produce a particular stylistic effect, but the sentences do not end in complete feet of the same sort, and the feet are broken up, the rhythmical effect is changed and that produces an impression that is typical of another style, not the one that relies upon those rhythms in which most of the speech has been composed.

Asperity (*Trachytēs*)

7 I said before that of those subtypes that create Grandeur and weight

255 the next after Solemnity is Asperity [or Harshness]. Discussion of that topic should follow here. Asperity and Brilliance too can be found to exist on their own, like Solemnity, but they can also be used to produce Florescence, as though they were subgroups of that style, [which is itself a subtype of Grandeur]. However, they are not subtypes of Florescence

in all those elements that produce a style, that is, thought, approach, diction, etc. They have certain elements that are peculiar to themselves and others that they share with Florescence. For example, certain thoughts and certain kinds of diction are typical of Asperity and Florescence, but the clauses that produce Asperity are not characteristic of Florescence. Likewise certain figures and kinds of clauses could make the style either brilliant or florescent, but the thoughts that produce Brilliance are not appropriate to Florescence. Because of this we are not discussing Florescence first, as though it were created through Brilliance and Asperity, as we did when we discussed Clarity and then dealt with the two subtypes, Purity and Distinctness, that create it. Rather, we shall discuss each of these three styles separately. For Florescence is created not only through certain elements that it shares with Asperity and Brilliance but also through some features that are characteristic of Vehemence, as will be clear when we discuss that style. So we must discuss each one separately. First of all we shall deal with Asperity, the opposite of which is Sweetness. For a harsh passage is bitter and very critical. Later we will discuss Sweetness and charm in the section on Simplicity, but now we must turn our attention to Asperity.

The thoughts that are typical of Asperity are all those that involve some open reproach of more important people by someone who is less important. I give you the following examples from Demosthenes:

If indeed you carry your brains in your heads and not trampled 256
down in your heels. . . . (7.45)

We are like men who have drunk mandragora or some other drug. (10.6)

And if you look at the noble dignity of the Council or at the Areopagus, hide your faces when you remember the verdict passed on Aristogeiton. (*Letters* 3.42)

And you, hamstrung and robbed of your money and your allies, have taken the role of servants and hangers-on, content if they hand over to you the Theoric or the Boidic [*sic*] Fund for your festivals. (3.31)

For you seem to me to have become completely slack and to be waiting to suffer some calamity, and although you see others suffering you do not take precautions. (19.224)

And surely it is not characteristic of wise or noble men to have abandoned their duty because of a lack of war-funds and then to bear such reproaches lightly. (3.20)

The approach of the last example is gentler than the others since it is stated in general and does not reproach anyone in particular, but the thought, nevertheless, is harsh. As far as the clauses are concerned, both of the last two examples are close to Florescence, as will be clear when we discuss that topic. This is not true, however, of the first examples, which are written in a purely harsh style. It is difficult to find clear examples of Asperity in Demosthenes, which is why I have tried to leave out none of those that are obvious. They are hard to find because generally he tones down passages of criticism by weaving into them certain other approaches, as he does in the following passage from the *Letters*: "To have treated such a man in this way would appear to me to be certain disaster, but it was not wickedness, but ignorance" (2.8). Here the thought of the sentence is harsh, but by presenting it as he does and by placing it in the context in which it appears, he has toned it down somewhat, although the next sentence, "You could absolve yourselves by changing your verdict," is also rather harsh. Likewise: "Oh, what could I say that would not seem to be less than true or a lie? Are you so careless, do you feel shame neither before others nor yourselves, because you exiled Demosthenes on the same charges on which you acquitted Aristogeiton?" (*Letters* 3.37). This is the sort of passage that, because of the hesitation, makes some amends for the criticism and gives the passage a gentler tone. In general you would find many such passages in Demosthenes and in other writers, although, as I said earlier, it would be hard to find many clear examples of Asperity in Demosthenes. For he uses such a style very rarely—unless you think that Vehemence and Asperity are the same style. That is not the case, as we shall show later, when we discuss how they are different from each other. Examples of unmitigated Asperity are, as I said, very rare in Demosthenes. There are, however, many examples in Aristogeiton, if you want to take examples from him, and many also in Dinarchus. But let this discussion of the thoughts that create Asperity suffice.

257

There is only one approach that produces Asperity, that is, to make a   258
reproach boldly and openly without toning it down with any of those
techniques that soften the harshness of the criticism. The best examples
of pure Asperity are those given a little earlier, where a harsh thought
has been presented in a harsh manner.

The diction that produces Asperity is metaphoric (or tropical), using
language that is harsh in itself. Examples from Demosthenes are "You
carry your brains trodden down in your heels" (7.45) or "You, Athenians, have been undone and you sit here reclining" (19.224) or "You have
been hamstrung" (3.31) or "ate it right up" (25.62) or "undermined, city
by city" (9.28) or "vandalizing and mugging Greece" (9.22). There are
others. These expressions are harsh because of the metaphorical nature
of the language, which itself is often harsh, as in expressions such as
atarpos or *emarpten* or *egnapse* and the like.[16] Likewise expressions
such as *perikoptōn* (vandalizing) and *ekneneurismenoi* (hamstrung) are
harsh, although less so than those mentioned earlier. This then is the
diction appropriate to Asperity.

Figures that produce Asperity are first of all those that involve com-
mands, such as "Hide your faces when you remember the verdict passed
on Aristogeiton." Secondly, points that are made by means of questions
seem harsh, as the following examples from Demosthenes show: "Then,
the Olynthians know how to provide for the future, but you, although
you are Athenians, do not?" (23.109) or "Do you not see that the poor   259
Olynthians have become a vivid and clear example of what I have been
saying?" (19.263) or "Are you deliberating, Athenians, when you have
Thebans on the island?" (8.74). For if one should overlook how this
thought is presented here and the fact that it is an example,[17] and should
imagine that Demosthenes is saying it directly, or for that matter anyone
else in reference to the topic under debate, rather than recalling what
someone else has said, it will be very harsh, especially because of the
figures used. Moreover, Asperity, on a second or third level of importance, uses almost all the figures, as is the case, I think, in all the other
types. But the ones mentioned above are most characteristic of it.

The clauses that produce Asperity are rather brief. In fact it is better
to call them phrases (*kommata*) rather than clauses (*kōla*), as in the
following examples from Demosthenes: "Will we not embark? Will we
not set forth? Will we not sail to his land?" (4.44) or "When then,

gentlemen of Athens, will we do what must be done? When what happens? When, by Zeus, there is some necessity? But now how should one interpret what is happening?" (4.10).

In a harsh style words should be put together in such a way that sounds clash and are dissimilar to those that precede and follow, and form metrical patterns that are inconsistent, so that there will be no hint of meter and no charm produced by the order of the words and no appearance of harmony. The effect rather should be unrhythmical, unharmonious, and grating to the ear. This effect is produced by a certain
260 sort of cadence. As we said in reference to the other types, a cadence of a certain sort combined with a certain kind of word arrangement produces the rhythm of the sentence. The cadences used in Asperity, like the arrangement of the words, should be formed from inconsistent metrical patterns, with the clauses ending sometimes in one kind of foot and sometimes in another. Thus the rhythm that is appropriate to Asperity is cacaphonous, as though there were no rhythm at all. This is the case in the vehement style (*sphrodrotēs*) as well, which we shall now discuss more fully, so that we can determine how it differs from Asperity. Sweetness is, in a general sense, the opposite of Vehemence, as it is of Asperity. But more particularly Modesty is the opposite of Vehemence. We shall discuss that, however, in our treatment of Character.

Vehemence (*Sphodrotēs*)

8 The thoughts that produce Vehemence, like those that produce Asperity, involve criticism and refutation. But Asperity is directed against more important persons than ourselves, or indeed the jurors or members of the Assembly, as we have pointed out. Vehemence, on the other hand, is directed against less important persons, such as our adversaries, or against people whom the audience would be delighted to hear criticized. Demosthenes uses this style against Philip when he says, "He is a barbarian, a wretched Macedonian" (9.31). He also uses it against other
261 people. This is the first way in which Vehemence differs from Asperity in thought. Because of this the reproaches are made more openly, almost like slanders, as in what is called "the commonplace."[18] You can treat inferior people in such a style, but you cannot deal with superiors in

that way. They can be dealt with harshly but not vehemently. Almost the entire speech of Demosthenes against Aristogeiton is an example of Vehemence, but it is especially clear in the following passage: "Therefore, will this man gain his release, this man who is the scapegoat, the public pest, whom anyone when he saw him would shun as a bad omen rather than address him?" (25.80). And you could find many other examples from the other speeches, such as "You disreputable scribbler" (18.209) or "but not a scandal-monger, a man who loafs in the marketplace, a wretched scribe" (18.127) or "Why, then, you wretch, do you spread slanders? Why do you compose speeches? Why do you not take a dose of hellebore?" (18.121) and "Your father was a thief if he was like you" (10.73). In general, as I was saying, there are thousands of examples of this in the judicial and in the deliberative speeches. These then are the thoughts that are characteristic of Vehemence. But if anyone should prefer to call them harsh or the harsh thoughts vehement, that is all right with me. They are different from each other because Vehemence is stronger than Asperity, and thus you would not be able to direct a vehement passage against someone more important than yourself, unless your audience would receive the criticism favorably. This is obvious from what I have said and is well known to anyone who is at all perceptive about public speaking.   262

The approach that produces Vehemence is almost the same as that which produces Asperity. That is, in a vehement passage one must make reproaches openly and clearly and in a straightforward manner without including in the passage any sentiments that tone down its severity. All the passages previously cited are good examples.

Similarly the diction that produces Vehemence is like that which produces Asperity. Here too it is a good idea to invent words that sound harsh, as Demosthenes does in the speech *On the Crown* when he calls Aeschines an "iamb-eater" (139) and a "porer over records" (209) and other such epithets. In harsh passages I have not found any examples of such coined words, and in this respect also perhaps Vehemence differs from Asperity.

The figures that produce Vehemence include, first of all, apostrophe or direct address, such as "They lodged with you, Aeschines, and you sponsored them" (18.82). A question is also an [appropriate form of] address to one's adversary. In addition to producing Vehemence it has an element of refutation about it. Thus such a figure is used in the case of assertions that cannot be contradicted, as the following from Demosthenes' speech *On the Crown*: "But what was it necessary that the city 263 do, Aeschines, when it saw that Philip was preparing to rule over and tyrannize the Greeks?" (66) or "Was it necessary that the city give up its reputation and its honor and place itself in the rank of Thessalians and Dolopians?" etc. (63). Expressions that point straight to something (*to deiktikon*) also produce Vehemence: "*This* wretched eater of iambs" (18.189). Or, having narrated various acts of Aeschines that furthered Philip's designs and that included "making false reports here in Athens," Demosthenes then brings forward the pointing expression (*deixin*) "*This* is the man who now grieves over the misfortune of the Thebans" (18.41). It is clear from this discussion that Vehemence differs from Asperity not only in reference to thoughts and to diction, as has been pointed out, but also in reference to the figures that produce it.

Perhaps there is also a difference in the sort of clauses that are appropriate. Clauses that produce Vehemence are not really clauses (*kōla*) but phrases (*kommata*), which is also true of Asperity. This is even more so in a vehement passage, which does not even use phrases, but tends to have pauses after single words, as in the following examples from Demosthenes: "the scapegoat, the pest" (25.80) or "but not a scandalmonger, a loafer from the marketplace, a wretched scribe" (18.127). There are other examples.

There is no need to discuss the cadence or rhythm that produces Vehemence, for that should be obvious from the previous discussion. Enough has been said in the discussion of Asperity, where the same principles apply as here.

The discussion of Brilliance will follow the treatment of Asperity and 264 Vehemence. In a certain way a passage that is quick-paced is the opposite of Brilliance. In particular, passages that are built up of short phrases (*kommata*) and have the tone of debate or, in general, dispute are the opposite of Brilliance, which we shall now discuss.

Brilliance (*Lamprotēs*)

9 Having treated Solemnity, Asperity, and Vehemence, we must now discuss Brilliance. Of those types that produce Grandeur and dignity

Brilliance is especially important. This type is necessary in a dignified speech for several reasons, but especially because a speech that is solemn and harsh and vehement also needs an element of luster, so that it will not be overly severe. I do not mean by this the kind of luster that is produced by adornment. That is characteristic of Sweetness and Simplicity. Nor am I talking about the kind that produces a beautiful effect through the care taken with the arrangement of words in the sentence. The latter kind of style is decorative and is often found in Demosthenes. It is nevertheless slight and does not produce elevation and Grandeur. To make the passage really elevated, therefore, you do not need the kinds of luster just discussed, but the kind that is truly dignified. That is Brilliance, which I will discuss now. We have already mentioned the kind of style that is the opposite of Brilliance in the discussion of Vehemence, where we said that it is conversational and argumentative, composed of short phrases, and generally quick-paced.

Therefore, a passage is brilliant with reference to the thought when 265 the speaker has some confidence in what he is saying, either because what he is saying is generally approved or because he has acted honorably or because his audience is pleased with what he is saying or for all these reasons. In general Brilliance is inherent in those acts that are remarkable and in which one can gain luster or, as Herodotus says (1.80), in which one can "shine." This is the case in the following passages from Demosthenes' speech *On the Crown*: "I did not fortify the city with stones and with bricks, nor do I consider that the greatest of my achievements reside in such things. But if you want to see the fortifications that I build you will find weapons and cities," etc. (299) or "This was the beginning of our dealings with Thebes and the first negotiation, since before this these men had reduced our attitude toward the Thebans to hostility and hatred and distrust. This decree caused the danger surrounding the city to disappear like a cloud" (188) or "Your ancestors did this, the elders among you did it when they saved the Spartans," etc. (98) or "You, therefore, Athenians, when the Spartans ruled by land and sea and were holding with governors and garrisons all the frontiers of Attica, as well as Euboea, Tanagra, and all Boeotia," etc. up to "you set out to Haliartus" (96). And there are many examples of such a style in the speech *On the Crown* because it is by nature dignified and brilliant. These thoughts, then, and those like them are characteristic of Brilliance.

266   The approach that is typical of real Brilliance is to introduce the thought directly, with confidence and dignity, without hesitation, using narration and not breaking up the narrative with digressions, if you are interested in consistent Brilliance. Suppose that Demosthenes had said: "This was the beginning of our dealings with Thebes and the first negotiation. This decree caused the danger surrounding the city to disappear like a cloud." That is completely brilliant. By breaking up the narration, however, and interjecting the clause "since before this these men had reduced our attitude toward the Thebans to hostility and hatred and distrust," he has used an approach that keeps the passage from being too brilliant. It does not have the same effect to speak the sentences without an explanation, as we wrote them above for the sake of illustration, and to break up the sentences with the explanation as Demosthenes does: "This was the beginning of our dealings with Thebes and the first negotiation, since before this these men had reduced our attitude toward the Thebans to hostility and hatred and distrust. This decree," etc. The same is true of the following example from Demosthenes: "A great advantage, Athenians, existed for Philip, for among the Greeks, not some, but all" (18.61). Here again he has broken up the narration with a contradiction and thus has prevented excessive Brilliance in the passage.

    It is also typical of the approach that produces Brilliance to speak noble sentiments nobly, as Demosthenes does when he says: "No, I swear it by those of our ancestors who fought at Marathon," etc. (18.208). He 267 could have said: "I advised you rightly to fight on behalf of the liberty of the Greeks. For those who fought at Marathon acted thus." This would have been stated in a noble way. But by using the oath he has made the expression even nobler and has produced a brilliant passage: "I did not make a mistake when I advised you to do this, no, I swear it by those who fought at Marathon," etc.

    The diction that produces Brilliance is the same as that which produces Solemnity. The figures appropriate to Brilliance are those that are comely, such as direct denials (*anaireseis*): "I did not fortify the city with stones or with bricks," etc. Indications of a fresh start (*apostaseis*)[19] also produce this effect: "This was the beginning of our dealings with Thebes," etc. And, generally speaking, to narrate facts without connectives (*asyndeton*), if the clauses are long, makes the passage brilliant, even if it is florescent in respect to the thoughts. Indeed Florescence (*akmē*), which we shall discuss next, is produced by means of figures and clauses that are characteristic of Brilliance, plus the other elements that create it. Moreover, one must realize that if you establish your proposition and state your basic point at the outset using an independent clause and then indicate the starting point, the passage will be less brilliant. If, however, you stretch out the sentence by immediately introducing a subordinate clause or some figure that by necessity expands the sentence, provided that the basic thought is not interrupted, in this way Brilliance is produced, as Demosthenes does when he says: "You, therefore, when the Spartans ruled by land and sea," etc. If he had not immediately introduced the subordinate clause "when the Spartans ruled 268 by land and sea" and thus by necessity expanded the thought, but had continued to use independent clauses, the passage would have been pure, but not brilliant. The following sentence is proof of this: "The Thirty Tyrants are said to have taken money from the Spartans to be used against those in the Peiraeus" (20.11). Even though it has been introduced without a connective, nevertheless, because it relies on an independent clause it is pure and simple, but nowhere brilliant. Such sentences also differ from passages that are brilliant in the following respect, namely that passages that exemplify Brilliance are not so much narrations of deeds as qualifications and amplifications of deeds. The pure style, on the other hand, which is almost the opposite of the brilliant, nevertheless, like the brilliant, indicates fresh starts (*apostaseis*), which are independent, with the subject in the nominative case, and it involves the narration of facts; however, it does not amplify or describe those facts, which is characteristic of Brilliance. The following sentences from Demosthenes, for example, are not brilliant for this reason: "There is a certain Sannio, the man who trains tragic choruses" (21.58) or "Once upon a time, in the good old days, we learn of Alcibiades" (21.43) or "The Thirty Tyrants are said to have taken money" (20.11). There are other examples. But enough concerning the figures that are characteristic of Brilliance.

The clauses that will make the passage brilliant must be rather long, and all the passages that we cited in our discussion of the thoughts that produce Brilliance exemplify this. The types of composition that produce Brilliance are the same as those that produce Solemnity, concerning which we have already spoken. But sometimes it is also possible to use

269   trochaic rhythms, which does not reduce the Brilliance of the passage, provided that the cadence at the end is one that is typical of Solemnity. Such cadences, coupled with long clauses, produce a rhythm that is solemn and brilliant, even though the metrical configuration of much of the sentence itself is composed of trochees.

Here we end our discussion of Brilliance. Next we shall discuss Florescence. The style that is the opposite of Florescence, as far as the thoughts are concerned, is the same as those styles that are the opposite of Vehemence and Asperity, and, in other respects, the same as those that are the opposite of Brilliance.

Florescence (*Akmē*)

10   Following the discussion of Clarity we showed in our comments how Solemnity and then Asperity and Vehemence and Brilliance are related to one another and how they add Grandeur to a speech by giving it some dignity and weight. Now we must discuss Florescence, which logically follows the treatment of Asperity, Vehemence, and Brilliance. As we said above, the styles that are the opposite of Florescence, as far as the thoughts are concerned, are the same as those that are the opposite of Vehemence and Asperity, and in other respects the same as those that are the opposite of Brilliance. There are several reasons why the treatment of Florescence must follow the discussion of those styles with which we have already dealt, but particularly because Florescence is generally created out of these, as we mentioned briefly in the discussion of Asperity. But we shall demonstrate this more clearly here in the section on Florescence, and what we mean will be clear from the outset.

270   The thoughts that produce Florescence and also the approaches are the same as those that are characteristic of Asperity and Vehemence. And the diction suitable for Florescence is that which is characteristic of Asperity and Vehemence with words that are typical of Brilliance mixed in, as in the following passage from Demosthenes: "For a terrible disease, gentlemen of Athens, has fallen upon Greece and it is oppressive and requires tremendous good luck and care on your part" (19.259). The metaphor, although it is typical of a harsh or vehement passage, has been uplifted in some way,[20] as happens in a brilliant passage and

here does not exemplify Asperity as much as it does Brilliance. But I think that we have discussed such words sufficiently in the section on Solemnity.

Also the figures that produce Florescence are those that one finds in Brilliance and Vehemence. For example, Florescence is created in the following sentences from Demosthenes in conjunction with a figure that is characteristic of Brilliance: "You have deserted, Athenians, the post at which your ancestors left you" (10.46) or "A great advantage, Athenians, existed for Philip" (18.61). For in each case he has indicated that he is making a fresh start (*apostasis*). This is true of the following examples from Demosthenes also: "Do not let anyone be acquitted or condemned because this one or that one wants it" (19.296) or "The Olynthians would now have many things to say, which if they had known them before, they would not have been destroyed" (9.68) or "As long as the ship is safe, whether it is a large one or a small one, then both the sailor and the pilot and every man without exception must be zealous, but when the sea wins, zeal is useless" (9.69). There is an additional element in these sentences that should be noted. Not only are they introduced by making a fresh start (*apostasis*) as in "A great advantage, Athenians, existed for Philip" or "You have deserted, Athenians, the post," but they are also built up, quite unexpectedly, by means of parenthesis (*epembolē*). Hence the sentence is more brilliant and the Florescence has more luster in it. Strictly speaking, this would have been an indication of a fresh start (*apostasis*), but if having established the proposition you state it at the outset of the passage, this is less obvious, as when Demosthenes says at the outset of the sentence "A great advantage, Athenians," etc. Here the indication of a fresh start (*apostasis*) has been expected by us and we see it. This is not the case in the following passage from Demosthenes: "By Zeus, we should have done this and not done that. The Olynthians would have many things to say," etc. (9.68).[21]

However, as I was saying, Florescence is created by means of figures that are characteristic of Brilliance. Direct addresses (*apostrophai*) and refutations (*elenchoi*), which are typical of Vehemence, would also create Florescence, as in the following examples from Demosthenes: "Was it fitting, Aeschines, that the city give up her reputation and her honor and place herself in the position of Thessalians," etc. (18.63) or "It is not necessary, Aeschines, to speak with folded hands, but to go on embassies

271

with folded hands" (19.255). And you should not be surprised if a direct address, even though we have said that it is a figure that is characteristic of Vehemence, also reveals Character in some way, as is the case with the following examples from Demosthenes: "And do not be angry with me, for I will not say anything nasty about you" (20.102). The thought

272 has been introduced in a such a way that it does not seem to have been said out of bitterness because of his opinion of the character of Leptines, but nevertheless it is vehement. Therefore it also reveals Character. Ironic statements make it clear that one can reveal character and be vehement at the same time, as in the following examples from Demosthenes: "How do your affairs stand thanks to these good men?" (3.27) or "She brought you up to be her pretty puppet, her marvelous bit-part actor" (18.129). There are thousands of other examples. The following from Demosthenes also both reveals Character and creates Vehemence: "Are you similar, Aeschines? And your brother? But in reference to the living, my good friend, must you judge living men," etc. (18.318).

These, then, are the figures that create Florescence. All the other elements of style, that is, clauses, word order, cadences, rhythms, are the same as in Brilliance. And here we end our discussion of Florescence.

But from what has been said someone might reasonably be at a loss as to the nature of the following sentences from Demosthenes: "Up to this point Lasthenes was called a friend of Philip," etc. (18.48) and "But the one who was annexing Euboea and preparing it as a base of operations against Attica," etc. (18.71) and other such sentences. Are they florescent or brilliant or both, which is probably the case? We would argue, just as we demonstrated in our discussion of Brilliance and then, likewise, in the section on Florescence, that on the whole Florescence

273 shares many traits with Brilliance, such as the fact that the clauses are long and that they use similar rhythms, which implies other similarities in reference to word order, etc.; and often we discussed the style, especially the use of figures that indicate a fresh start (*apostatika*). Thus if we should say that in this style there are elements blended from both Brilliance and Florescence, sentences such as "Up to this point Lasthenes" fall into the same category and appear nonetheless florescent, if indeed Florescence generally shares many characteristics with Brilliance. And the thoughts of sentences such as "Up to this point Lasthenes was called a friend of Philip" and "But the one who was annexing

Euboea and preparing it as a base of operations against Attica" seem to be vehement since they are spoken against individuals, which is also characteristic of Florescence. It is the combination of the figures used and the clauses, which are typical of Brilliance, that, with the thoughts, create Florescence. Hence someone might ask: Why, then, is it necessary to say that in these sentences Brilliance and Florescence have been blended together, since by nature these must always be mixed when the passage is florescent?

But one must realize that, first of all, we are saying that in these examples Florescence and Brilliance have come together, not that Asperity or Vehemence appear together with Brilliance, which is what normally produces Florescence. The combination of Florescence and Brilliance does not create Florescence: thoughts and approaches that are typical of Asperity and Vehemence, combined with the diction and clauses that are characteristic of Brilliance, plus any other element that may be mixed in, create Florescence. Therefore they are not reciprocally implied. Florescence always has in it some element of Brilliance. But Brilliance does not have in it any element of Florescence, unless someone argues unfairly that the features peculiar to Brilliance (long *kola*, *apostatika*, etc.) are ambivalent because they are found in both types and can just as well be transferred from Florescence to Brilliance or vice versa.[22] That is nonsense. It is obvious by mere perception that these elements are characteristic of Brilliance and that Florescence does not have any basis for existence in itself, but that the mixture of elements typical of Asperity and Vehemence, on the one hand, and of Brilliance, on the other, creates Florescence. Therefore, as I was saying, they do not necessarily imply one another. A passage that is florescent generally also has elements typical of Brilliance and Vehemence or Asperity or both. But a passage that is harsh or vehement or even brilliant is not necessarily also florescent. Asperity, Vehemence, and Brilliance can exist on their own, even apart from one another. One could say that it is possible to create Florescence out of a thought that is typical of Asperity or Vehemence, or out of a clause that is typical of Brilliance. But these are not necessarily characteristic of Florescence. Therefore, to those who argue that these sentences are florescent, whereas I argued that in them both Florescence and Brilliance have been mixed, first of all, as I was saying, one must realize that Florescence is not created out of Florescence and Brilliance, but from those elements that I discussed above. The sen-

274

275 tences under discussion, that is, "Up to this point Lasthenes" and "But the one annexing Euboea," and others similar to them, involve a combination of styles, beginning with the thoughts. For the thoughts are typical of Brilliance and Vehemence, but probably more so of Brilliance, if one examines them with real knowledge. But let us recall what we said about the kinds of thoughts that are typical of Brilliance: they are those in which the speaker is discussing something about which he is very confident. Surely, then, if Demosthenes wanted to establish in that passage that if Athens had taken Philip's side, it would not have been beneficial to the city, he proved his point in reference to both nations and cities, using as examples the Thessalians, who were being governed by tetrarchs, and others, as he does in the following passage: "For indeed if after his victory Philip had withdrawn immediately and then had kept quiet, wronging none of his own allies or the other Greeks, one could perhaps have blamed and accused those who had opposed his enterprises. But if he destroyed the honor and the power of all," etc. (18.65). As I said, he has made his point in reference to cities and nations. And to establish his thesis also from the experience of individual men, he says: "No one spends money to benefit a traitor" (18.47). Then, wanting to prove this, he gives many clear examples that are well known to all. Since he speaks with confidence, he uses a brilliant style. Indeed I do not know whether we have a better example of Brilliance than the sentence "Up to this point Lasthenes was called a friend of

276 Philip," etc. The clauses are quite long. The orator is very confident about what he says. And the repetition (*epanaphora*) of the paired phrases "up to this point . . . until" produces a marvelous beauty. But we shall discuss that more precisely in our treatment of Beauty.

Now we must return to our discussion and to the point that we were making, namely, that because of the reasons stated above the thought of this sentence is typical of Brilliance. It is certainly not Demosthenes' task in this passage to accuse Euthycrates and Lasthenes and the other traitors, but to establish the proposition that he had stated. For this reason the sentence is typical of Brilliance. But there is obviously also an element of Vehemence, because the sentence seems to be directed at persons, namely the traitors. And yet a speech against a traitor should not be like this, that is, simply narrative and not very vehement, although there is, even as it stands, some element of Vehemence.

Given the nature of the thoughts in this passage, therefore, even if they were the only element under consideration, one would probably say that here Brilliance and Florescence have been combined. But it is obvious that there are other elements that are characteristic of Brilliance as well. If the thought is typical of Brilliance—and it is, as we have clearly demonstrated—then it is only natural that other elements, such as the approach and the figures, would also be brilliant. But because Florescence is also produced from these elements, we must say here that such features of style are common to them both.

What I have been saying applies also to the sentence "But the one annexing Euboea." Everything that Demosthenes says in this passage is a confirmation and proof of the fact that Philip has broken the peace. And since Demosthenes is sure that his arguments are clear and convincing, he uses a brilliant style. But, nevertheless, here there is more Florescence, just as in the other sentence there was more Brilliance. Here he is clearly speaking against a person and not simply narrating facts without really making an accusation, as he does in the other sentence. Moreover, the passage seems to be more florescent because he uses against Aeschines a rhetorical question as a means of refutation. This figure, although it is really most typical of Vehemence, can be used in a florescent passage, but not in one that is brilliant. Also, this sentence does not use extended subordinate clauses, but seems to chop up a single thought with phrases that are stitched together (*symplokai*), which is not typical of Brilliance or, indeed, of Florescence, but rather of Vehemence. But Vehemence is totally unlike Brilliance, whereas Florescence is closer to it. This also makes the sentence appear to be more florescent than brilliant. And if this sentence also exemplifies Abundance or, rather, a thought that is fully developed, that is another question.

So much concerning Florescence. Now we shall discuss Abundance. This is the last of the types that produce Grandeur. The opposite of Abundance is Purity, as we said in the discussion of Clarity.

Abundance (*Peribolē*) and Fullness (*Mestotēs*)

11 After the discussion of Clarity we proposed to talk about Grandeur and weight and dignity and how these can be added to a speech, and we

278   said that Solemnity, Asperity, Vehemence, Brilliance, Florescence, and last of all Abundance produce these qualities. Therefore, having discussed all the other types that produce Grandeur, we must now talk about Abundance. An understanding of this is very important for several reasons, but especially because Demosthenes uses it more often than the other types that give Grandeur to a speech. We shall discuss later why this is so. It is not a good idea to state this before we have demonstrated what Abundance is, which we shall do now. And we have already said in the discussion of Clarity that Purity is the opposite of Abundance.

There is Abundance with reference to the thought whenever you add something extraneous to the subject matter of the speech, such as when you discuss a larger genus (*genos*) to which a species (*eidos*) belongs, as Demosthenes does in the following passage: "A wicked thing, Athenians, an informer is a wicked thing, and this little man is by nature a cunning rogue" (18.242). Or you can mention the undefined as well as the defined, as Demosthenes does when he says, "In this trial I am inferior to Aeschines in many ways, but there are two, Athenians, of great importance" (18.3). Or you can discuss the whole to which a part belongs, as Demosthenes does here: "Although this whole Acropolis is sacred and although its area is so large, the inscription stands on the right next to the great bronze statue of Athena" (19.272). The Acropolis is not a general class of which the place on the right of the statue of Athena is a species, nor is Demosthenes here mentioning something undefined in

279   conjunction with what is defined, but he is here describing the whole to which a part belongs. Adding a point and then breaking it down into its component parts, even though that does not involve mentioning something that is undefined, also creates a certain abundance, as Demosthenes does when he says, "And there are two important matters, the one is this, the other is that" (18.3) or "The three worst reproaches are directed against us: that we seem to be envious, ungrateful, and untrustworthy" (20.10). Or if you should say, "He said two things, this and that," you would create Abundance. There are in Demosthenes many examples of this as well as of the other features discussed above.

It is clear that such additions are also characteristic of Distinctness, as well as producing Abundance. If the audience know in advance what they are going to hear, that creates Distinctness, and if unnecessary

statements are made that creates Abundance. And you should not be surprised if Distinctness, which seems to be the opposite of Abundance, is able to be created through the same technique, that is, by adding a statement and then breaking it down into its component parts (*kat' athroisin proslēpsis*). These kinds of style are not so opposed to each other, as is the case with certain others, that they are not able to coexist. They are not, in other words, like heat and cold or death and life or night and day and other such opposites that cannot exist together. On the contrary, not only is the nature of these styles such that they can coexist but, in fact, a speech is especially admirable when it is constructed out of opposing types that are well blended together. But such mixing and blending of styles is difficult, and hardly any of the ancients, except Homer, does it as admirably as Demosthenes. For how would it not be difficult to mix Purity with Abundance, and Clarity with what is excessive and full, or to mix the insignificant with the solemn, the grace-   280
ful with the grand, the simple with the vehement, the pleasant with the harsh, beauty where audacity is needed, or the ornamental with the persuasive, or the concise and the argumentative, and what is everyday, though not cheap or base, with what is brilliant, or the persuasive and that which expresses truth and what comes from the heart with what is florescent, and whatever other kinds of style with those that seem by nature to be their opposite? I do not know whether there is anything in speech-making more difficult than this, especially if one is not only to use all the individual styles properly but also to mix and blend them together in an appropriate way. We shall wait until we discuss the approach that is characteristic of Force to illustrate this more clearly with examples. Now I shall say only what I have said, so that no one should be surprised that Abundance and Distinctness can be created through the same technique, for this is not really an important aspect of them. These types are not even opposite to each other, but it is, in fact, always necessary in all passages that are abundant, that is, when the topic is amplified and dealt with in a full way, that something of those elements that create Distinctness be present. This is necessary in order that the speech not become confused and unclear, as we showed in the discussion of Distinctness.

I return to the beginning of the discussion of Abundance. As I was   281
saying, whenever someone adds an idea that is extraneous, this creates

Abundance as far as the thought is concerned, as we demonstrated—or whenever the bare facts are not narrated on their own, but circumstances related to them are added, such as the place of the action, the time, the cause, the manner, the person involved and what his intention was, and other such matters. This is what Demosthenes does in the speech *Against Meidias*: "I promised to outfit a chorus" (13). When? "Two years ago." Where? "In the assembly." Why? "Because a chorus master had not been established and, therefore, there were arguments and reproaches." How? "As a volunteer." What state was Demosthenes in? "I was not very rich," he said, "and to try to undertake something beyond one's resources may have been an act of madness" (69). This point is peculiar to the person concerned. What was his intention? "Because of ambition." Abundance is created because of these additions primarily in the thought. All of these elements could be amplified in other ways, which would make the speech even more abundant as far as the thought is concerned. For example, if he had said, "I promised to outfit a chorus although I was poor," this would have been a bare fact about himself. How does he amplify it? First, by comparing himself with others, "since no one was undertaking to do this," and then by expanding it even more, "not even among the rich," and then by amplifying it even further, "although I was not immune from the other public services, but had performed many of them, both by making voluntary contributions and by outfitting ships." Generally if you want to expand each detail you could discover many arguments and examples and many things that are defined and undefined that would do so. Not only do those techniques discussed above create Abundance, but you can take arguments from every source, such as bringing in comparisons, or opposites, or discussing the general class, or a particular example, or by describing the whole, or a part that belongs to the whole, or by using the argument from the greater, the equal, or the less. These perhaps are not really additional details, but rather kinds of proof;[23] at least enthymemes and examples are created by means of such arguments. But a discussion of this would entail a section on proofs.

282

Moreover, Abundance is created in the thought if one not only narrates what was done but also what the consequences would have been if it had not been done, and what had to be done so that such and such would happen, as if we should say: "Having let pass and overlooked everything else, he accomplished those things for which he had been paid" (18.149). In any case these are the ways in which Abundance can be created in the thought.

The following approaches create Abundance. The first is to reverse the order of the facts and to relate the second first, which will force you to insert what happened previously in a parenthesis, as Demosthenes does: "But when we returned from this embassy for the oaths, the one about which a scrutiny is now being held" (19.17). Then he inserts parenthetically what happened first: "without realizing anything, either great or small, of those advantages that were promised or expected when you made the peace," etc. up to "we came before the council." By inverting the order of the facts Demosthenes creates Abundance in the approach, in order that, as I was saying, he might have to insert a parenthesis, as here, or to add what happened first, as he does in the following passage: "But in the hostel in front of the temple of the Dioscuri (if anyone of you has been to Pherae, he knows where I mean) the oaths were administered" (19.158). Up to this point there has been a parenthesis in "if anyone of you has been to Pherae, he knows where I mean." What follows is fastened on, and in this way too he has created Abundance: "when Philip was coming here with his army." Then he qualified this, which also creates Abundance by amplification (*auxēsis*) of the thought: "shamefully, Athenians, and in a manner unworthy of you." Whether Demosthenes has also created some other effect by describing this action in a judgmental way is another question. Also, since he has interjected the phrase "if anyone of you has been to Pherae, he knows where I mean" at the beginning of the sentence, he has not only created Abundance but also Rapidity (*gorgotēs*). Moreover, since the thought is broken up, this also seems to be typical of the sincere style. But we cannot discuss that now.

Therefore, to invert the order of the facts is an approach that is characteristic of Abundance, as has been said. And to put the reasons for making a statement (*kataskeuē*) and the proofs that support it and the amplifications of it before the statement (*protasis*) itself, as Demosthenes does in the speech *On the Crown*, also produces Abundance. In that speech (102) he makes a specific statement: that he proposed a law concerning the provision of ships that was beneficial to the city. He gives us reasons for making this proposal: that the poor were no longer

283

to be treated unjustly and that the rich were no longer able to gain exemptions by making small contributions, which kept the city from taking advantage of many opportunities. But consider how he intro-

284 duces the reasons for making the proposal and the amplification of them before the proposal itself: "When I saw that your navy was falling apart and that the rich were gaining exemptions by making small contributions and that those citizens who were only moderately wealthy or even poor were being ruined and that the city, therefore, was not able to take advantage of opportunities that offered themselves, I proposed a law," etc. There is also quite a lot of Force in this sentence, as we shall show when we discuss that topic. The sentence is similar, in fact, to the following: "If it were being proposed, Athenians, to deliberate about some new matter" (4.1). Here too you have in the proemium a proposition, namely, that one who is young must be listened to even if he speaks first; and reasons are given—among others, that at many meetings of the assembly concerning this issue the older men have not said what needed to be said. But the reasons are again stated before the proposition itself. Isocrates does the opposite of this in the *Archidamus*, and thus makes the speech less abundant and not at all forceful, when he says, "Perhaps some of you are amazed that I, who heretofore have followed the customs of our city," etc. (1). These then are the approaches that create Abundance.

In my opinion there is not a particular kind of diction that is characteristic of Abundance, as there was for the other types. I suppose, however, that you could say that the use of parallel constructions that say the

285 same thing in different ways is typical of Abundance, as Demosthenes does in the following sentences: "What will we say? and what will we utter?" (8.37) or "Seeing these things, Athenians, and considering them, I propose a decree" (18.27) or "There are trials and legal processes involving severe and heavy fines" (18.14) or "Then the people were lord and master of all their possessions" (13.31). There are thousands of examples of this in Demosthenes. Some critics, scrutinizing these examples in their typical fashion, have said that they produce Abundance.[24] But we have already expressed our opinion about this. The use of synonymity might involve some element of refutation or amplification or clarity or some other feature of style, and if it also exemplifies Abundance, that is really not a question of diction. No type of diction in

and of itself produces Abundance, but by combining words with one another one indirectly produces an impression (*emphasis*)[25] of Abundance. "What will we say?" is not abundant in and of itself, nor is "What will we utter?" or any of the other examples given above. But putting them side by side has perhaps indirectly created a certain impression (*emphasis*) of Abundance. This is certainly not caused by the diction, but rather, more probably, by the approach. Sometimes we put whole thoughts that are similar in parallel constructions, especially when we want to linger upon an idea, but in my opinion that is not really characteristic of Abundance either, but rather of Force, which is created through the approach. For we dwell on points and elaborate those that are favorable to us, as Demosthenes does in the speech *On the Crown* 286 when he says: "Was it fitting, Aeschines, that the city give up her reputation and her honor," etc. (63). He repeats this thought more than four times in the same passage, and he generally uses the same figure, that is, a rhetorical question combined with a direct address. Because the thought is one readily acceptable to his audience he lingers upon it and forcibly presses it upon his opponent with repeated questions that do not give him a respite. Demosthenes does this with arguments that are favorable to him, but in dealing with points that do not support his case he uses a different tactic. Those he treats in as few words as possible. All this will become clear in our discussion of Force.

Thus we linger upon those arguments that are favorable to us, and that is a question of the approach. To say "What will we say? and what will we utter?" (8.37) involves the use of a certain approach, which we could reasonably agree also creates Abundance. Hence the use of synonymity (*epimonē*) properly belongs to the discussion of the approaches that create Abundance, although it does not produce Abundance in every passage where it is found. But because of the arguments given above, we shall agree that sentences such as "What will we say? or what will we utter?" or "And yet when he appeared to have done this and to have acted in this way toward me" (18.14) exemplify Abundance. In the second example the parallel phrase "to have acted in this way toward me" is synonymous with the first, as is the word "utter" in the first example.

Figures that produce Abundance are, first of all, those that generally 287 imply a second thought or even a third one. In addition to these there are others, which we shall discuss individually. But first we shall discuss those figures that cannot establish thoughts on their own, but, as I said, bring other thoughts in with the first. An enumeration (*aparithmēsis*) is one such figure, as when an orator says, "First I will deal with this, and then I will deal with that." This also produces Distinctness and Simplicity, if there is a parallel construction in close proximity. But if the parallel construction is delayed, this produces Abundance. If repetition (*epanalēpsis*) is also involved, the repetition makes the passage distinct, whereas the delayed parallelism generally produces Abundance. This is what happens in Demosthenes' speech *On the False Embassy*. He says: "First, gentlemen of Athens, in order that no one of you will be amazed when he hears me narrating some episode" (25). Then, having discussed many matters in what is almost a parenthesis, he repeats himself: "This was the first and most important reason why I narrated these facts" (27). Then he introduces the parallel phrase that one necessarily expects from the figure that he used earlier: "And what is the second reason?" etc.

Thus an enumeration, or any figure that resembles an enumeration, produces Abundance, such as the following passage from the speech *On the Crown*: "First of all, Athenians, I pray to all the gods and goddesses that whatever goodwill I have shown to you, you will show to me" (1). Then he adds, "Secondly, what is in your own interest." To introduce arguments in the order of their importance (*kata protimēsin*) also creates this effect, as Demosthenes does when he says, "Mainly I think that it is beneficial to the city to annul this law, but also I am sympathetic to the son of Chabrias" (20.1).

Figures that involve fictitious suppositions (*kath' hypothesin*) also imply other thoughts,[26] especially if the supposition is cast in the form of a division (*meta merismou*), as Demosthenes does: "If our project had already reached the point, Aeschines, that the Thebans could gain no advantage by learning of it, why has it not happened?" (19.42). Then he adds what one expects: "But if the project has been thwarted because they knew about it in advance, who let out the secret? Was it not this man?" Moreover, whenever anyone makes a supposition, even if there is no division of the proposition, he will have to state another thought that necessarily follows, although he will not create Abundance in the same way as he would have if he had divided the proposition. In the following passage from Demosthenes, for example, it is not clear

288

what conclusion must follow, since there is no division, and, consequently, there is less Abundance: "If I intrigued with Philip to prevent
the city from making a peace in conjunction with a union of all the
Greeks" (18.22–23). Then he states the necessary conclusion: "It was
left to you to break silence."

The use of subordinate clauses (*plagiasmos*) also implies other
thoughts, as when Demosthenes says, "Since the Phocian war was
going on," etc. (18.18). Then comes the main clause that necessarily
follows: "You were thus disposed." Abundance has been created in this
passage not only because of this figure, but also because of the thought
and the approach [27] and several other figures, such as the parenthesis
"not because of me, for I was not in politics then" and the enumeration
"at first you were so disposed" and many others. But the use of subordinate clauses creates the most Abundance, as in the following passages
from Demosthenes: "Although there are many speeches, Athenians, at
almost every meeting of the assembly," etc. (9.1) or "Since, there being
no chorus master established for the Pandionis tribe," etc. (21.13).

There are thousands of examples of this technique in Demosthenes,
and of Abundance in general. There is really no passage in his speeches
that does not exemplify Abundance, unless, I suppose, someone should
take a sentence out of context and then say that it is not abundant but
pure. The following passage, for example, seems to exemplify Purity:
"There is a certain Sannio, the man who trains tragic choruses. This
man was convicted of shirking his military service" (21.58). But if you
look at the passage closely, you will find that the phrase "he was in
trouble" immediately follows. How is this typical of Purity, except in the
use of an independent clause without subordination? [28] In fact, how
could one argue that the whole passage that follows does not exemplify
Abundance? Therefore, as I was saying, there are thousands of examples
of Abundance in Demosthenes. Indeed, even in the private speeches
this type of style is often used, although I think that there is more need
for Purity in those speeches because most of them involve an argument
from Character. The reason he uses Abundance so often—I promised
that I would deal with this question here—is that Demosthenes was
eager to give Grandeur and dignity to his speeches. Of those types that
generally create Grandeur in his speeches, however, almost none are
really appropriate in the private speeches except Vehemence. And even

289

the vehement passages are not strong but are toned down somewhat. None of the other styles, however, would be appropriate. In private speeches no one would use Asperity or Solemnity or Brilliance or Florescence.[29] There are places where Vehemence could be used in a way that is quite appealing, as Demosthenes does in the speech *Against Boeotus* when the adversary is addressed as "O troublesome Boeotus" (34). You could find many examples of this. But Abundance could have been used almost everywhere even in the private speeches, as is demonstrated by the fact that such is the case. In the public speeches the other types that create Grandeur can be used because the subject matter is appropriate for them. This is especially so if the speaker himself is dignified and has a noble reputation, as in the speech *On the Crown*. If he speaks in general terms when he makes reproaches he can then use florescent passages, as Demosthenes does in the *Philippics*. But not even in public speeches is it possible to use the other styles such as Solemnity or Asperity or Vehemence or Brilliance or Florescence as often as one uses Abundance.[30] That is the reason Demosthenes, who understood oratory perfectly, uses Abundance so often in comparison with the other styles. But this is a digression, and we must return to our discussion of the figures that produce Abundance.

290

A figure that involves expanding the sentence with a causal explanation (*to epitrechon ek tou parasynaptikou*) also implies other thoughts: "Since there was no longer a regular meeting of the assembly because they had already been used up" (19.154). The use of an expression that requires subordination (*hypostasis*) also implies other thoughts: "I *so* clearly refuted Philip *that* his own allies rose up and agreed" (18.136) or "*Whatever* benevolence I have shown to the city and to you all, *so much* will I receive from you in this trial" (18.1). There are other examples. Divisions (*merismoi*) also have the same effect: "Whatever Philip seized and held before I entered politics and became a public orator, I shall pass over. But what he was prevented from doing from the time when I entered public life, this I shall discuss" (18.60).

291

Since the figure that is called division, or partition, is found in almost all oratory, not only in Demosthenes, I should say something more about it. Any division generally produces an indirect expression (*emphasis*) of Abundance because it implies something else. It creates either obvious Abundance or, indirectly, an impression of it (*emphasis*), and it also does something else. When the second part of a division (*antapodosis*) is delayed, Abundance is obviously created, as in the following example from Demosthenes: "Therefore, to discuss Philip's strength and by these arguments to urge you to do what is necessary" up to "and whatever other topics I could discuss" (2.3–4), which is the second part of the division. This example is also full in addition to being abundant. Fullness is nothing other than Abundance taken to an extreme, or what one might call "abundant Abundance." We shall discuss this more clearly a little later and give more compelling examples. At any rate, as we were saying, a division with the second element delayed creates Abundance. If, on the other hand, the second element is given very quickly, this produces Rapidity, as the following examples from Demosthenes' speech *On the Crown* show: "It was evening, and a messenger came to the presiding councilors" (169) or "He accuses me, but indicts this man" (15). If, however, parallel phrases had been employed throughout (*kata syzygian*), the passage would have been beautiful and finely wrought, as in the following example from Demosthenes: "From the expenses of the chorus masters, pleasure is given to the spectators for a small part of the day, but from the abundant funds spent on war equipment, safety is given to the city for all time" (20.26). Here the two independent clauses 292 that are made up of paired phrases as in a strophe and an antistrophe create a parallelism. And in this sentence the even balancing of the clauses, which have the same number of syllables (*parisōsis*), in addition to the division by pairs of parallel phrases, has also created Beauty.

Divisions make the passage full, if there are divisions within divisions. In Demosthenes' *First Philippic*, for example, he begins the speech with a division: "If concerning some new matter, gentlemen of Athens, we were now deliberating," etc. (1). But before giving the phrase that is the responsion to this one, he has inserted another division: "if they had said anything that pleased me, I would keep silent; otherwise, I myself would attempt to say what I think." Then he gives the phrase that corresponds to the first one cited above: "but since we are deliberating about matters that they have discussed often." Because of this double division the passage becomes full. Thus whenever divisions are inserted into other divisions this makes the passage full, which also happens when a division is itself divided: "Therefore, this decree, by giving security to Charidemus, who is directing the affairs of king Cersobleptes, and by instilling fear and dread of being accused in the commanders of the other kings" (23.10). Then, before breaking off the thought, he has attached another division that is dependent upon the first one: "it makes those kings weak, and the one who stands alone strong." Thereby he has made the passage full.

293   Thus, generally speaking, fullness is created whenever figures that create Abundance are used in conjunction with one another, either by means of insertion or by attaching one onto another, as I have already said. This also happens when figures that produce Abundance are somehow welded together, such as when a division is combined with syntax that requires subordination or some other combination is used, either by insertion or attachment, as we demonstrated above. For, as I said, fullness is simply expanded Abundance. If several figures that create Abundance are used together in the same passage, through parenthesis or some other technique, the passage becomes full. And if such passages are spoken clearly and not in a confused way, they produce tremendous vigor and power. Demosthenes is outstanding in this respect. But enough about division and fullness.

We said earlier that not only those figures that involve or, as it were, "drag along" other thoughts produce Abundance, but also certain others, which we must now discuss. A figure that involves negation and affirmation (*kata arsin kai thesin*) creates Abundance by making the passage complete, as the following phrases from Demosthenes illustrate. He says, "not as one who would sell your interests" (19.12). Then he gives the affirmative of this: "but as one who would guard the others." We did not put this with those figures that drag other thoughts along with them, because a negation can stand by itself and an affirmation does not necessarily follow it: "At first you were so disposed, not because of me, for I was not then in politics" (18.18). Here nothing affirmative follows the negation.

294   A figure that involves negation and affirmation creates Abundance by making the passage complete. Copulative constructions that involve a negation (e.g., "not only this, but also that") also create Abundance, since thoughts that are expressed in such a way seem somehow to have been treated fully: "Not only would you receive it gladly if someone came forward with a plan that was well worked out, but also I consider it part of your good fortune" (1.1). Moreover, a figure that involves

packing many thoughts into one sentence (*to kata systrophēn schema*) makes the passage very abundant: "If when we came, having brought aid to the Euboeans," etc. (1.8) or "The one doing those things by which I might be captured," etc. (9.17).

We have demonstrated sufficiently in the previous discussion of fullness, as well as in our treatment of Purity and in several other places, that parentheses, or any technique that brings the thought to a stop before it is completed and inserts other thoughts, are characteristic of Abundance, and we gave many examples of this. But one must also recognize that these parentheses can be used to relieve the dullness sometimes found in narrations, by breaking up the passage and, in the process of breaking it up, making it more vigorous and rapid. The following passage from Demosthenes illustrates this. He begins: "Since the Phocian war was going on" (18.18). Then he breaks off the narrative and inserts the phrase: "not because of me, for I was not then in politics." Then he returns to the narrative: "At first you were so disposed," etc. The following sentence from the orator illustrates the same technique: "Therefore, this man was the first of the Athenians to perceive, as he said in his speech, that Philip was plotting against the Greeks" (19.10). And generally speaking, if the parentheses are short rather than long, this makes the passage rapid rather than abundant: "He appears, 295 as indeed he proves, to be worthless" (2.5). Do you see how quick and rapid the sentence is? This effect has been created by the insertion of the short parenthesis "which is also true." There is also here an element of Abundance, just as, when the parenthesis is long, there is generally also an element of Rapidity, although long parentheses tend to make the passage more abundant than rapid. Thus, we have discussed sufficiently the various elements related to the thoughts and the approaches and the figures and the diction, if there is one (see the previous discussion), that create Abundance.

We are not able to say what kinds of clauses or word order or cadences or rhythms are typical of Abundance. Abundance can use all the clauses, so to speak, and all the rhythms that are typical of the other types of style, and all the kinds of word order and all the cadences. Thus all these styles admit elements that are typical of Abundance, except perhaps Purity. Purity is destroyed if Abundance is used, and, generally speaking, as I said in my discussion of that style, Purity is the opposite of Abundance. Consequently, in many respects, if not in all, Abundance and Purity are created out of elements that are completely different from one another. But one should not be surprised if it is possible to cast a thought that is abundant in a form that is pure, or vice versa. It is possible for one who seems to speak in a pure style to be abundant as far as the thoughts are concerned by arranging everything in its proper order, and, conversely, for one who seems to speak abundantly to produce a thought that is pure and simple. I think that we have shown this clearly enough in our discussion of Purity.

296

Carefully Wrought Style (*Epimeleia*) and Beauty (*Kallos*)

12 The discussion of a carefully wrought style and Beauty in and of itself would naturally follow our treatment of Clarity and the dignity that is produced by means of Grandeur. For a speech that is clear and weighty and dignified obviously also needs an element of Beauty and rhythmical harmony so that it will not become unharmonious or rough. It is obvious that a style that is carelessly constructed and unrhythmical and pays no attention to the order of the words is the opposite of Beauty. This kind of style may be useful, for example in the creation of Asperity and Vehemence, but that is another question. Here we must discuss Beauty and a carefully wrought style.

The Beauty that is found in a passage would properly be the kind that is created by all those elements that produce all the types in it, that is, thoughts, approaches, diction, etc. It must be harmonious and well-tempered, with a certain uniform quality of character appropriate to the type throughout the entire passage, just as complexion in the body. What I have just said is true whether one chooses to work in one particular style or to blend them all together, in whatever way they lend themselves to combination, to pursue a varied and typically Demosthenic kind of style that is really suited to political discourse, or to combine only certain styles with others. To use an analogy with the human body, Beauty generally consists of symmetry and harmony and proportion in the various parts and limbs of the body, combined with a

297

fresh and healthy complexion. That is also how the style is produced, whether you mix all the types together or concentrate on each one individually—for these are, as it were, the "parts and limbs of the body." At any rate, if the passage is going to be beautiful, whether that Beauty is varied or of one kind, there must be a certain harmony and proportion that exists, either among all the styles that are being used, if the Beauty is of the mixed kind, or among all the elements that make up the style being employed, if it is of the simple kind.[31] It is also necessary that a certain healthy complexion, as it were, bloom in it, a uniform quality of expression appearing throughout, which some critics naturally call the complexion (*chrōma*) of the speech.[32] This is the kind of Beauty that Plato seems to me to mean when he says (*Phdr.* 264c) that a speech must have a head and extremities and middle parts that are in proportion to one another and to the whole body, but that these individual parts must not be thrown together in a confused way, even if, taken individually, they are quite beautiful. A speech, even though its individual parts are beautiful, cannot be beautiful itself, if they are not arranged with harmony and proportion. That is why Socrates criticizes the "Erotic Speech" of Lysias (*Phdr.* 234eff.). He says that the thoughts are not arranged in a harmonious way, although he does not criticize the thoughts themselves or the style. Socrates himself uses the same thoughts in his own speech, and he warmly praises Lysias' diction, saying emphatically that the speech is very polished in its use of language and has been nobly expressed by the orator. But we must postpone any discussion of Lysias' oratory, either in its entirety or only of the "Erotic Speech," and return to what we were discussing before. The Beauty of a speech would properly consist of those elements that we discussed earlier.

However, in creating Beauty there are certain stylistic elements that are clearly more effective than others. These are like adornments applied from without for the sake of embellishment. Some critics, in fact, are willing to give to these stylistic features alone the name "Beauty." Isocrates, indeed, says in the *Panathenaicus* (2), when he is discussing balanced clauses (*parisōsis*) and other such stylistic devices, that it is these elements that make the audience cheer and applaud. But Demosthenes also appears to have used them often, since they are no less necessary than those types of style that have already been discussed and that will

298

be discussed later. We shall now deal with these elements that comprise Beauty.

First, one must realize that this kind of Beauty is really just a question of style and those elements that are related to diction, such as figures of speech, clauses, word order, and cadences, and the rhythm, which is produced by a combination of those features just mentioned. There are no thoughts, in and of themselves, or approaches that are typical of Beauty, except perhaps the use of striking words and turns of phrase, which we shall discuss later in our treatment of Simplicity and Sweetness. Now we must discuss diction, following the pattern that we have agreed upon.

The diction that creates Beauty is entirely the same as that which creates Purity. Rough and metaphorical words are vivid and perhaps have some other effect, as in the phrases "I did not suspect that he was corrupt and had sold himself" (19.13) or "hamstrung" (3.31) and other such expressions. But they are not beautiful in the sense in which we are now using the word. That is why Isocrates, who was especially concerned about Beauty, used these kinds of metaphors very seldom. Generally it is short words and words composed of only a few syllables that produce what we have called a carefully wrought style and Beauty, such as in the following passage from the speech *On the Crown*: "I am concerned about how you ought to receive what I have to say" (*peri tou pōs akouein hymas emou dei*, 1).

The figures that create Beauty are those that call attention to their ornamental nature and show clearly that the style has been embellished, such as balanced phrases (*parisōsis*), which are frequently found in Isocrates. They can also be found in Demosthenes, although there are not so many and they are not so highly developed as they are in Isocrates. In fact strict parallelism and balance is rare in Demosthenes, although one sometimes finds it: "He thinks that it is necessary to send aid to the city and to take vengeance on his own behalf, and I shall try to do this" (22.1).[33] We are able to find no other example of a balance so elaborately worked out in Demosthenes.[34] We have discussed why he has deliberately used such a carefully worked out style in the proemium of this speech in our discussion of the speech *Against Androtion*.[35] It is obvious that Demosthenes uses this kind of style rarely. I do not mean that he uses balance rarely, but that he uses it in moderation and gen-

299

erally keeps the parallelism from becoming too strict. He does this either by breaking up the clauses with a parenthesis or by breaking the balance at the end of the clauses or by using parallelism throughout the entire clause, but not using rhyming syllables at the end—although he does do this in the passage from the speech *Against Androtion* cited above, and Isocrates does it often. Demosthenes, however, does not generally use such strict parallelism, but usually disturbs the balance in these three ways: either by breaking it up with an insertion or a parenthesis, as I mentioned, or by changing the order of the words, or by balancing the whole clause. The following is an example of the way in which he breaks up the parallelism with an insertion: "To have lost so many possessions in the war anyone would attribute to our negligence, but that we did not suffer this long ago"—and here he adds an insertion —"and that the alliance with these men offers us some compensation if we are willing to take advantage of it"—and then he gives the clause that is parallel to the second half of the first clause—"I would attribute this good fortune to the benevolence of the gods" (1.10). Here he breaks up the parallelism with an insertion. And here is an example of how he changes, at the end of the clause, the order of the words in a parallel construction: "And this was the first ruse of Philip on the embassy, and such was the venality of these men" (18.31). If he had said, "Therefore, on the embassy we saw a ruse in Philip, and we saw venality in these men," his clear intention would have been to produce a passage of Beauty. [But his goal is to persuade.] Thus he has changed the order of the words [so that the parallelism will not seem overly artificial]. The following sentence is similar to this: "Nothing true did he report, and he prevented the people from hearing the truth from me, and not one of those orders that you gave did he execute, and he wasted time" (19.8). [Demosthenes] could have placed the balanced elements at the end of each phrase: "Nothing true did he report, and that the people hear the truth from me he prevented, and time he wasted, and not one of the orders that you gave did he execute." This would have made the sentence remarkably more beautiful, but much less persuasive.[36] Thus he avoided this kind of strict parallelism. There are many examples of this in Demosthenes if you want to look for them. Another is: "Since I made this proposal then and was seeking what was beneficial to the city, not to Philip" (18.30). He avoids strict parallelism because he deeply under-

300

301

stood the art of oratory. Isocrates, on the other hand, would not have avoided it. In fact he would have forced thoughts that are not really parallel into a balanced construction because he was more concerned with Beauty and a carefully wrought style than with persuasion and truth.

Demosthenes also often uses parallelism throughout an entire clause. Such a practice is typical of Beauty, but it also has something rapid and truthful about it: "Therefore, granted that you agree that it is legal to accept gifts, that one feels gratitude for them, do you indict this as illegal?" (18.119). By means of three generally parallel clauses he has introduced one that is shorter than the others: "do you indict this as being illegal?" In addressing his opponent directly he has made the passage divinely beautiful, but also rapid and vehement.[37] Isocrates uses many such parallelisms, but he does not combine them with direct address. In fact apostrophe is generally not used in Isocrates.

Finally, let me say that the parallelism can be at the beginning or at the end [of words],[38] as in the following examples from Demosthenes *prosēkei prothymos* ("it is appropriate that you hear eagerly"), and from Plato, "and when Pausanias stopped (*Pausaniou de pausamenou*), for the sophists teach me to make jingles" (*Symp.* 185c). And I have already demonstrated how parallelism can be created at the end: *tei te polei boēthein ōieto dein kai dikēn hyper hautou labein*," etc. (Dem. 22.1).

Thus parallelism creates Beauty, as I have said. A specific kind of parallelism is one consisting of repetitions at the beginning of a clause (*epanaphora*): "Up to this time Lasthenes was called a friend of Philip, until he betrayed Olynthus. Up to this time Timolaus was so considered, until he destroyed Thebes" (18.48). He repeats the same phrase at the beginning of each sentence. This figure differs from assonance in that it is not a single syllable that is repeated or perhaps two, but a whole phrase or a whole word. I suppose that epanaphora is also an instance of assonance, since a whole phrase or word is repeated, which involves the repetition of syllables, but assonance is not epanaphora, since it does not involve the repetition of words.

You should not be surprised if the preceding example also has an element of Brilliance or Florescence in it. For in every way there is a relationship between Brilliance and Beauty and between Florescence and Beauty, since techniques associated with Beauty are used in both these styles. Things that are florescent and graceful—either bodies or whatever[39]—are generally also brilliant and beautiful. The reverse, however, is not true. Something can be beautiful without being florescent or brilliant.

Finally, repetitions used in short phrases make the passage rapid, but not beautiful: "Coming forward (*prosiōn*) to the Council, and coming forward to the people" (19.10). Here too the fact that the corresponding member of the division is given quickly creates Rapidity.

Another figure that produces Beauty is antistrophe, which is the opposite of epanaphora because the clauses use the same word at the end rather than at the beginning. This differs from assonance in the same way as epanaphora differs from it. The following are examples: "If a man gets something and keeps it, he has tremendous gratitude to fortune, but if he loses it through neglect, he also loses his sense of gratitude to fortune" (1.11) or "Some business is being transacted that seems to be to your advantage: Silent is Aeschines. Something has been hindered and some regrettable incident has taken place: Present is Aeschines" (18.198) or "As for carrying on the affairs of war quickly and opportunely he is far superior, but as for those pacts that he would like to make with the Olynthians, he is not superior" (1.4). This figure is rare in Demosthenes. Moreover, like epanaphora, if it is used in short phrases it makes the passage rapid, but does not create Beauty: "taxiarchs from you, hipparchs from you" (4.27). Whether repetitions, either epanaphora or antistrophe, also make the passage vivid is another question.

Epanastrophe is also a figure that creates Beauty. This involves beginning a clause with the same word with which the preceding clause ended: "Certainly he would not have been able to indict Ctesiphon because of me, but me myself he would not have indicted, if he thought that he could win a conviction" (18.13). And the very contrived quality of a passage is obvious whenever a writer makes the final syllable or syllables of one word the beginning of the next, as Thucydides does when he says, *Samia mia naus* ("one Samian ship," 8.16) or *autika boē ēn* ("Straightway there was a shout," 3.22) or as Homer does when he says, *Prothoos thoos hēgemoneue* ("swift Prothoos was leader," *Il.* 2.758). The following passage, however, although it represents an epanastrophe, is not like those cited above nor does it appear to be so

303

304

carefully constructed, since he does not repeat a syllable or a word, but a whole phrase: "I will go against him, even if his hands are like fire, /Even if his hands are like fire, and his rage is like flashing steel" (*Il*. 20.371–372).

Another figure that creates remarkable Beauty in a vivid way is the one that is called climax. This is rare in Demosthenes. In fact it appears only once or twice. A climax is nothing more than an extended anastrophe: "I did not say this without making a proposal, nor did I make a proposal without going on the embassy, nor did I go on the embassy without persuading the Thebans" (18.179). That the corresponding elements of the division are given quickly, the clauses are short, and the frequent denials are handsomely stated has also made the passage rapid, but that is another question. The handsomely shaped nature of this sentence, and the direct denials themselves, are in some way characteristic of Beauty. But even if that were not the case, it is very difficult, as I have often stated, to find any passage in Demosthenes that exemplifies only one type. He is the most varied man of all, and in almost any passage of his speeches you would find everything, so admirably does he mix and combine all the types. They all nearly pervade one another in his works, and, as if they had been melted together, they have combined to create a style that is the noblest of all and the most suited to practical oratory, the style that we call the Demosthenic. We shall discuss practical oratory more specifically when we have finished our treatment of the types in general.

Divisions of paired thoughts that use clauses of equal length (*hoi kata syzygian merismoi dia tas isokōlias*) also produce Beauty, as we showed in our discussion of Abundance. Hyperbaton [the separation of elements that naturally belong together] has the same effect, unless it creates a parenthesis rather than a transposition of words. The following example illustrates what I mean by a hyperbaton created by a transposition of words: "Having chosen instead of a life of safety the honor —things that no other king of Macedonia ever achieved—of achieving these things" (2.15). And the following is an example of hyperbaton created by means of a parenthesis: "He appears, as indeed he proves, to be worthless" (2.5). We have already said in our discussion of Abundance what effect an insertion such as a parenthesis has: if it is short it creates Rapidity, if it is longer it creates Abundance, and if there are many of them that creates fullness.

Novel means of expression (*schēmata kainoprepē*) also create Beauty: "And you, the people" (3.31) or "if not even because of one other reason" (23.195) instead of "because of no other" or "The Thessalians have never not betrayed any one of their allies, not even one" (23.112). Moreover, affirmations created by means of two negatives (*hai dia dyo apophaseōn ginomenai kataphaseis*)[40] are typical of Beauty: "nor being unwilling to fight" (Homer *Il.* 4.224) instead of "willing" or, in Demosthenes, "It is not unclear that Leptines . . . " (20.1). Here instead of saying "it is clear" he has said "it is not unclear."

The figure that is called polyptoton [the use of the same word in various cases and genders] is also characteristic of beauty, if it is used in different clauses: "*This* was the beginning of our negotiations with Thebes and the first settlement. *This* decree made the danger surrounding the city disappear like a cloud," etc. (18.188). If, however, polyptoton is used in phrases, it creates Rapidity, but this is not really far removed from Beauty: "*These* were your leaders: *in them* you trusted, *by them* you might be deceived" (19.298). These, then, are the figures that create Beauty.

The types of clauses (*kōla*) that naturally produce Beauty are those that are moderately long if the words flow smoothly and there is no clashing of vowels [hiatus] in them, as in the works of Isocrates, where not only the clauses but also the whole discourse is held together by harmonious sounds, so greatly was he concerned about euphony and Beauty. These things as I was saying, really create Beauty in the clause. But also those clauses that are short but closely connected with one another seem to show careful workmanship and a certain degree of ornamentation, though subdued and not ostentatious. This happens when the clauses are woven together, in the manner of insertions, in such a way that the thought in each is not completed, but they must all be taken together: "Thus we must consider not only how Leucon, a man whose enthusiasm for this grant comes from his sense of honor, not from need, will not be treated unjustly, but also whether another man treated you well when he was prosperous, but has now come to need the exemption that he received from you then" (20.41) or "This is not unclear, Athenians, that Leptines, and anyone else who speaks on behalf of this law, will say nothing fair about it, but he will mention some unworthy men who use their exemption to shirk their public responsibilities, and he will use this argument a great deal" (20.1). You see how

307

short all the clauses are, except the last ones, in each example and how the insertions in some way do not seem to be insertions and appear to

308 have been put there as a natural consequence of what precedes rather than as unnecessary comments. This is not like saying, "He appears, as indeed he proves, to be worthless," or any of the other examples that we gave. In the passage just quoted there is more Rapidity, although there is also an element of a carefully wrought style, whereas in the examples given earlier, conversely, the style is more carefully wrought, although there is also an element of Rapidity. There are many other examples, in all the speeches of Demosthenes, of such Beauty and of this sort of carefully wrought style. This is especially true of the speech *Against Leptines*, which is very carefully constructed and very beautiful. We have discussed why this is so in our treatment of the speech itself.[41]

From the preceding discussion it should be evident what kind of word order is needed to produce Beauty. First, it must avoid the clashing of vowels [hiatus]. Secondly, the word order should produce metrical configurations that are very similar to meter. Thirdly, the meter suggested must fall into feet that are appropriate to the passage and to the kind of style that we are aiming at. There is one meter that is typical of Solemnity, as we said in the discussion of that style, and others that are characteristic of the other types, as we pointed out when we discussed each one of them. But whatever else it needs, a very beautiful passage requires great care in the placement of the words. It is in this respect that the carefully wrought quality of the passage and the remarkable embellishment that has been lavished on its composition are most obvious. Therefore, when we compose a beautiful passage, we especially need to use a rhythm that is close to meter, although it should not be too obviously metrical, like a line of poetry, for in prose that is a defect. As I

309 intend to treat this question more fully elsewhere, I ask that no one be offended by the minuteness of this discussion. I realize that anyone who is going to discuss any aspect of rhythm and of those elements that make a passage beautiful must be particularly accurate and minute. But now we must return to our discussion. As we were saying, as far as the word order is concerned, the first requirement of a passage that appears in some way to be metrical and that makes that impression on the ear is that there be no hiatus in it. Secondly, the feet from which the rhythm is composed must be related to one another and must not produce an

impression of Asperity by being mutually incompatible.[42] And thirdly, and most importantly, the words that create the rhythm must not have the same number of syllables or take the same length of time to pronounce or have the same accent. Some words should be short, and some should be long. Some should have one accent, and some should have another. The words should be put together in such a varied way that long words are found side by side with short ones, and vice versa. It is this kind of word order that is most typical of a carefully wrought and beautiful style.

Stately cadences are not suitable in a very beautiful passage.[43] These are too solemn and are appropriate only to a sort of solemn beauty, as in the following phrase from Demosthenes: *ekdedykenai tas leitourgiās* ("to have shirked their public responsibilities," 20.1). The cadence here, since it is composed of a long word with a final long syllable, is solemn and stately, for in this passage Demosthenes was concerned that the sentence not seem simply beautiful. The following passage from the same speech also has an element of the very beautiful, although it also seems stately in a way because the cadence ends in a long syllable: *kai toutōi pleistōi chrēsetai tōi logōi* ("and he will employ this argument especially," 20.1). Here he brought the clause to an end with a rather short word, and the completion of the thought brought the rhythm to an end—for the thought has been completed and is stately. But the word in which the thought ends is not typical of a stately cadence since it is short. It does, however, end in a long vowel, which is typical of a solemn rhythm. The rhythm is completely stately when the thought comes to a firm halt with a long word that has a long final syllable, as in the following example: *hōst' ex hapantōn rhaidian tēn tou sympherontos hymin hairesin genesthai* ("And so from all things the choice of what is beneficial to you is easy," 1.1). But the rhythm is not stately, but rather, as it were, suspended and disconnected, or limps,[44] in a way opposite to that just discussed, when the thought is not yet completed, but is somehow interrupted in the middle, and the cadence ends in a short word and has a short syllable at the end or next to the end, as in the following example: *egō d' hoti men tinōn katēgorounta pantas aphaireisthai tēn dōrean tōn adikōn estin, easō* ("But I will pass over the argument that it is unjust to strip all of this grant because you make charges against some," 20.2). You see the same phenomenon in the

310

following examples from this same speech (20.1): *esti d' ouk adēlon touth' hoti Leptinēs* ("This is not unclear, that Leptines . . ."); *kan tis allos hyper tou nomou legēi* ("and if someone else speaks for the law"); *dikaion men ouden erei* ("he will say nothing fair"). All these represent rhythms that are not stately but limp along, as I said earlier, and these are useful in a beautiful passage. For by not coming to a forceful halt they make the cadence graceful. Consider also the following example: *hōmologēsa toutois, hōs an hoios te ō, synerein* ("I agreed to support them, as far as I was able," 20.2). Here the thought has come to a firm halt, but the rhythm is not stately. Since the orator wanted the sentence to be graceful, he used the word *synerein*, which has a short syllable next to the end, at the end of the clause, rather that its synonym *syneipein*, which has a long syllable in the next-to-last position and thus would have made the rhythm stately. I think that he did this on purpose so that the impression that the cadence makes on the ear would not be the same as it would have been if he had ended it with two long syllables, which is typical of a stately rhythm. But whether the rhythm is stately or not (I do not want to contradict Dionysius completely, who seems to have worked out something of a stylistic theory), [45] it is obvious that it is characteristic of Beauty. Such a cadence is even more remarkable if the final word is monosyllabic, as in the following examples: *peri tou pōs akouein hymas emou dei* ("concerning how you will hear what I am going to say," 18.1), or *Thettaloi de oudena pōpote hontina ou* ("The Thessalians have never not betrayed any one of their allies, not even one," 23.112). Verses and poems are a very cogent proof of this. Indeed those epic verses that end in a monosyllabic word are somehow more graceful and musical but not more solemn, as the following examples show: *eti d' ambrosiē nyx* ("and still immortal night," Homer *Il.* 7.433); *karē tamoi allotrios phōs* ("a foreigner cuts my head off," *Il.* 5.214); *Apollōn Artemidi xyn* ("Apollo with Artemis," *Od.* 15.410). There are other examples. So much, then, about the kind of Beauty that can be added to a passage for the sake of ornament.

The style that is called graceful and charming does not involve this kind of Beauty, but the kind that is called Sweetness or Simplicity. This will be clearer when we discuss those styles. But now, following our treatment of Beauty, we must discuss Rapidity.

311

Book 2

Rapidity (*Gorgotēs*)

1 In previous discussion we considered how a beautiful and clear speech can be created and how weight and dignity can be added to it. Such a speech also needs Rapidity, so that not only will its Grandeur and Beauty shine forth clearly but it will also be rapid. That which is flat and carelessly constructed is the opposite of Rapidity.

Rapidity is seen in the style and in the approach and in the other elements that we have been discussing, except the thought, unless someone should say that pointed and clever thoughts are typical of Rapidity. But we shall discuss those in the section on Simplicity and Subtlety as well as in our treatment of Force. As far as the diction is concerned, whatever it may be, it contributes little to Rapidity. There is really only one approach that creates Rapidity, and that is the use of short clauses that develop the thought quickly. This effect is produced mainly through the figures and types of clauses that are used, but word order, cadences, and rhythms also play a role. As I said, there is no thought that in and of itself creates Rapidity, unless one should say that pointedly clever and subtle thoughts are typical of Rapidity. We shall discuss these, as
we said, in our treatment of Simplicity and Force. But now we shall deal first with the approach that produces Rapidity, which is similar to the one that produces cleverness and Subtlety, although not the same.

As we were saying, there is only one approach that creates Rapidity, and that is to use quick replies and concise objections: "Why did you send them at that moment? To seek peace? But we were all at peace. To stir up war? But you yourselves were discussing peace" (18.24) or "Yes. He says so. But look at the noble claim of Cephalus, that he was never indicted. Fortunate was he indeed. But why should a man who was often indicted," etc. (18.251) or "Are the Byzantines ill-fated? Of course. But nevertheless they must be saved, for that is beneficial to Athens" (8.16). These passages are also in some respects clever and pointed. We shall discuss more precisely in our treatment of Force the provisional concession of an adversary's viewpoint (*syndromē*) or agreement to his arguments (*synchōrēsis*) and what the various types of concession are and when each of them should be used.

Direct address (*apostrophē*) seems in a way to be an approach, as in "They turned to you, Aeschines, and you received them" (18.82), but it appears to me to be more a figure than an approach. But whether it is a 314 figure or an approach, it is one of those elements that create Rapidity in a speech, especially if it is used frequently. Shifting one's attention now to the jurors, now to the opponent or someone else, gives movement to the passage and makes it rapid. In any case this is the approach, or the approaches, characteristic of Rapidity.

There are figures that are generally agreed to be rapid and concise by nature and are used to create Rapidity in a passage. These can be employed to offset the flatness (*hyptiōtēs*) that often necessarily appears in a speech. We shall discuss these first.

The use of parenthesis (*schēma to kath' hypostrophēn*) can offset the flatness of a passage and is especially useful in narrations. Demosthenes says, for example, "He was the first of the Athenians to perceive Philip" (19.10). Then he breaks off the thought with a parenthesis: "as he said then, when he made a speech." Then he returns to the narrative: "[Philip] plotting against the Greeks." Likewise he says in another passage, "When the Phocian war began"; then he inserts a parenthesis, "not because of me, for I was not then in politics"; then he picks up the narrative, "at first you were so disposed" (18.18). The passage that follows this one exemplifies the same technique. Some have called this the "interweaving" figure (*schēma kat' epiplokēn*).[1] The figure that involves "overrunning" (*to epitrechon schēma*) can also offset the flatness of a passage: "Since the tribe of Pandionis had not appointed a chorus-master, now two years ago" (21.13). This figure also creates Abundance, 315 as do parentheses, if they are long, but less so than the figure just discussed. But we explained this in our treatment of Abundance.

These, then, are the remedies, as it were, for flatness, and they perform the same saving function as Distinctness does in Clarity. Distinctness sorts out ideas that are confused, with a view to producing Clarity, as we showed in our discussion of that style. Likewise these figures raise up a passage that is flat and languid and make it rapid. The following observation is also similar to comments that I made when I was discussing Clarity. There I said that Purity alone can make a passage clear, but that there is a need for Distinctness as well, to set it back on the right course, if ever the passage should become confused. Likewise here, it is a concise style that especially makes a passage rapid, but if the passage should become flat, as sometimes happens, there is a need for the figures discussed above to raise it up and give it life. For a concise and rapid style is created mainly by means of figures and rhythms. Moreover, one must keep the following points in mind. Sometimes a passage is concise, but does not seem to be so. Sometimes it seems to be concise, but does not really treat the topic concisely. And sometimes it is both. That is, it is concise and seems to be so. We shall give examples of this when we discuss each of these more fully.

Now we shall deal with those figures that are necessarily concise and rapid.[2] The following are of this kind. First of all there is asyndeton, or lack of connectives, used in conjunction with short phrases or words: "He came to the council, a decree was proposed" (24.11) or "Amphipolis, Potidaea, Methone, Pagasae" (1.9). Frequent and slight variations (*exallagē*) in a list have the same effect: "Having first taken Amphipolis, after this he seized Pydna, likewise Potidaea, then Methone in turn, afterwards he attacked Thessaly," etc. (1.12). Short divisions with an answering clause also have the same effect: "It was evening certainly, but a messenger came to the councilors announcing that Elateia had been taken" (18.169). Anaphora and antistrophe used in conjunction with short phrases also make the passage rapid: "Against the laws you are calling him, against yourself you are calling him" (Aeschin. 3.202)[3] or "taxiarchs from you, archons from you" (Dem. 4.27). Frequent, short interweavings (*symplokai*)[4] have the same effect: "Matters serious to my mind, gentlemen of Athens, and important to the city, concerning which you are deliberating, to discuss which I have come forward" (10.1) or "The fathers of you, Spartans, and of you the elders" (Thuc. 2.11). If there are many of these interweavings, but the thought is not completed and does not come to a halt in each one, but all are encompassed into one periodic sentence, there will nevertheless be an appearance of concision and even of moderate Rapidity, though the passage will be more abundant than rapid:[5] "But Euboea this man annexed and made it a base of operations against Attica, and he occupied Oreus," etc. up to "was he acting unjustly and breaking the treaty and violating the peace or not?" (Dem. 18.71). But now I must return to our discussion.

These, then, are the figures that produce Rapidity. These also surely create a style that appears to be concise, but is not really, as well as one

316

317

that both appears to be concise and is so in reality. However, these figures do not create a style that is in fact concise but does not seem to be so. To produce that impression you need to use subordination (*plagiasmos*) and concise oratorical periods (*ta kata systrophēn*)[6] and other such devices. By means of these figures much is said in a very few words, although we do not make it obvious that we are treating the matter under discussion concisely. We shall give examples of each of these to clarify our point.

The following passage illustrates a sentence that is concise but does not appear to be so: "Although there are many speeches, Athenians, at almost every meeting of the assembly," etc. (9.1). This sentence produces the effect mentioned because of the use of subordination. The following is an example of a concise oratorical period: "How could the one who orders the Spartans to give up Messene, if he hands over Orchomenus and Coroneia to the Thebans, be considered to have done this because he thought that it was just?" (6.13). In both of these examples much has been said in a very few words, although the sentences do not appear to be concise. There are thousands of examples of this in Demosthenes.

The following is an example of a passage that seems to be concise but is not so really, but in fact is abundant, which is the opposite of concise: "The one annexing Euboea and setting it up as a base of operations against Attica," etc. up to "by doing these things" (18.71). In this sentence Demosthenes seems to be saying a lot and to pass quickly from one topic to another, which produces an element of Rapidity and an impression of conciseness. But in fact he does not really say very much and does not really pass quickly from one topic to another. He lingers upon the same topic, which is typical of Abundance, and that is the opposite of Rapidity and concision. Here general classes are mentioned with particular examples, and wholes with the parts that make them up, and undefined concepts with defined ones, and other devices are used that create Abundance.[7] He adds each detail as if it were an independent fact, weaving them together and making transitions from one fact to another. Thus many things seem to be said, although in fact there are really only two topics discussed: the situation in Euboea and the plight of Byzantium. If you insisted, I would probably agree that there might be more, but there are certainly not as many topics discussed here as there appear to be. This impression is created by means of "interweavings" (*symplokai*). There are thousands of examples in Demosthenes of passages that do not treat the matter at hand concisely, but that seem to.

The following is an example of a passage that is concise and also seems to be so: "Matters serious to my mind, Athenians, and important to the city, concerning which you are deliberating" (10.1). But such a passage is rare in Demosthenes. 319

In our treatment of the approach that is characteristic of Force we shall discuss why Demosthenes uses conciseness sometimes in one way and sometimes in another and how it should be used. An understanding of that matter is really more relevant to that topic, since to know when and where and against whom and how one must use the various kinds of conciseness is an integral part of the approach that is associated with Force. But we must return now to our discussion of Rapidity. We have dealt with the approach and the figures that make a passage rapid. From our discussion of the figures that create Rapidity what we shall say next about word choice and clauses should be obvious.

Diction, as I said, of any particular kind, makes a small contribution to Rapidity, but short words are more suitable. The clauses that produce a rapid passage also must be very short.

The word order that creates Rapidity is one that rarely or not at all involves hiatus. A truly rapid passage must not have any gaping holes, unless there is some need for Asperity. The rhythm should consist of trochees or pairs of trochees. There are in tragedy many vivid examples of the effect that trochees have, for there the speaker often seems to be in haste when the meter is trochaic. There are also examples in Menander. Archilochus demonstrated this with even more Clarity and Rapidity. His tetrameters [measures of four double feet] seem to be more rapid and more prosaic than those of other writers, because they are composed of trochees (*trochaioi*). The rhythm literally runs (*trechei*) in these passages. In Demosthenes exact trochaic measures are not found even in rapid passages. But as I have often pointed out, in his speeches no single kind of style can ever be found in any passage, since he is constantly varying his style, applying a rhythm, for example, or an approach or some other feature of oratory that is typical of Rapidity, or of another style, to solemn thoughts, or vice versa. And yet the following sentence from Demosthenes probably does gain somewhat in Rapidity because a 320 trochaic rhythm is used from the outset: *hḗspĕrā mĕn ḡar ēn, hēkĕ d'* *ăngellōn tĭs hōs tŏus prŭtănĕis, hōs Ēlătĕiă kătĕilēptăi* ("It was evening certainly, but a messenger came to the councilors announcing that Elateia had been taken," 18.169).

The cadence that creates Rapidity is one that naturally ends in a trochee and is not stately. A rapid rhythm cannot be stately. We have fully discussed stately rhythms and those that limp, as it were, and are disjointed, in our treatment of Beauty.

Character (*Ēthos*)

2 We have shown in the preceding discussion how a clear and dignified and beautiful and rapid passage is produced. Discussion of Character must follow now. Although the other types of style are important, it is very useful to know how this ethical kind of style is produced and to be able to create it in order to give some quality that reveals Character to the entire speech, if that is necessary. It is also important to know how to blend it into all the styles that have already been discussed, such as Vehemence or Solemnity or Beauty and the others. In this discussion by "character" I do not mean simply the revelation of Character that necessarily appears throughout the whole speech, like the complexion of a body, but also that which is naturally combined with the other styles such as Vehemence, Asperity, and all the others. The first kind of revelation of Character that I mentioned, that which naturally appears throughout the whole speech, involves attributing suitable and characteristic words and arguments to certain persons, such as generals or politicians, or to general categories of people, such as the gluttonous or cowards or the avaricious or people who exemplify other traits.[8] We shall learn what kinds of style are appropriate to what kinds of people in our discussion of Force. But the kind of revelation of Character that we are now discussing, in all its various manifestations, can be employed anywhere in the speech like the other styles such as Solemnity or Asperity. And, like these, the various styles that reveal Character can be useful even when they are employed only occasionally, as often happens in Demosthenes. What I am talking about will be clearer when you have understood my discussion fully.

Character in a speech is produced by Modesty and Simplicity. In addition to these, truth and an unaffected manner, as they are revealed in the speech itself, also reveal Character. Indignation is also an element that expresses Character, although it is not as important as Simplicity and Modesty and truth and an unaffected manner. And Indignation cannot be observed alone, as can the other types, but must be present in conjunction with Simplicity or Modesty or one of the other styles that   322
reveal Character. We shall demonstrate this more clearly when we discuss each of these. First we shall deal with Simplicity.

Simplicity (*Apheleia*)

3   The thoughts that produce Simplicity are generally the same as those that are characteristic of Purity. Thoughts that are common to all men and occur to everyone, or that seem to occur to everyone, and that contain nothing deep or complex are obviously simple and pure: "Consider me a villain, but release this man" (19.8). It is generally agreed that pure thoughts are usually simple as well, and vice versa. Some people who are unaffected and childlike to a certain extent, not to say silly, are considered simple, but that is a special usage of the word. That is the impression produced, for example, when someone discusses certain events or tells a story, although that is totally unnecessary and no one has asked for it, as Anacreon often does or Theocritus in the pastoral poems, or many other writers: "I am serenading Amaryllis, and my goats are grazing on the mountain," etc. (Theoc. 3.1).

Since the examples that we gave in our discussion of Purity were typical of contentious political oratory, as is also perhaps the case with the example given earlier, "Consider me a villain, but release this man,"   323
and since we did not cite examples of pure and simple thoughts in other kinds of prose writing, we should discuss these somewhat more fully here. For I do not make a distinction between thoughts that are typical of Purity and those that are characteristic of Simplicity. In other words, some pure and simple thoughts are quite appropriate to political oratory, some are less so, and some are not appropriate at all. The latter would be those thoughts that are really peculiar to Simplicity, although, as I said, they are also pure. These are those thoughts that one hears in the mouths of little children, as I said, or men who are childlike or women

or country people or, generally speaking, anyone who is simple and guileless: "How handsome Granddaddy seems to me, Mother" (Xen. *Cyr.* 1.3.2) or, as Cyrus says of the Assyrians, "They are bad men themselves, and they ride bad horses" (Xen. *Cyr.* 1.4.19). Don't you see how simple the utterance is? Another example is: "The murmuring is sweet, goatherd, as is the pine over there" (Theoc. 1.1). There are many such examples in almost all pastoral poems, as there are in Anacreon. In

324 Menander you would also find innumerable examples, spoken by women and young men in love and cooks and similar characters. And, generally speaking, since all characters such as gluttons and farmers fall under the head of character writing, they must exhibit a style that reveals Character. All of them, or most of them, consequently, must exhibit a style that is simple. It should also be noted that if one is portraying a person of the kind specially called a "character," thoughts that are pure and simple are necessary and useful, but they are otherwise not suitable in political oratory.

Thoughts that in some way seem to border on the trivial are also simple. These are found whenever someone discusses trite and trifling matters, as in the speech against Stephanus, who was charged with perjury: "She poured handfuls of nuts over him" (45.74). The following example is similar, "to pick bare the rose garden" (53.16), as are the passages in the appeal *Against Eubulides* where Demosthenes says that Eubulides' mother sold ribbons in the marketplace (31.35). There are many such passages in the private speeches, and even more in Lysias. In public speeches they are rare, and they are usually introduced with some apology. For example, the phrase "He revels without a mask" is lifted above the trivial by the addition of the phrases "the dreadful Kyrebion" and "in the processions" (19.287). The following is another example: "But how did your mother practice daylight nuptials in a shed near the

325 statue of the Hero of the Splints and bring you up to be her pretty puppet, her marvelous bit-part actor?" (18.129). This is of the same general kind, even if it has been introduced with Vehemence — for the topic is trivial. However, the euphemism "daylight nuptials" as well as the Vehemence and the irony and the other features of style that it exemplifies make it more acceptable. Similar is the passage "Squeezing the brownish-red snakes" up to "names that the old ladies called you" (18.260). But Demosthenes apologizes for the passage in a sense and

distances himself from what he says by adding that Aeschines was called such names by old ladies. There is another passage that some critics have crossed through or deleted because it is so trivial, and perhaps they are right to do so: "She wandered about all summer shouting 'baked beans,'" etc.[9] Such passages as this might be appropriate in private speeches, but in a public speech, or one that should be as dignified as a public speech, because it deals either with a person or a topic of public interest, they have no place.[10] Similar too is the passage in the speech *Against Neaera*, which has also been questioned by some critics: "She plied her trade through three openings."[11] This is extremely vulgar, even though it seems to be vehement.

Thoughts that involve proofs (*epicheirēma*) that are constructed out of comparisons with animals are also simple: "The ox strikes with his horn, the horse with his hoof, the dog with his mouth, the boar with his tusk" (Xen. *Cyr.* 2.3.9). And if a speaker were to take his comparisons 326 from plants, he would produce a similar effect. These, in fact, have an even greater element of Simplicity and are close to Sweetness, which is why such comparisons are so commonly found in the poets. In the poets these comparisons also involve an element of Grandeur, which should not be surprising. They do not use a large number of such comparisons at a time, as in the passage quoted, but rather choose just one. This keeps the general tone of the passage from becoming simple. Moreover, poets are naturally concerned not only with what is pleasant but also with what is grand. Thus through diction and figures of speech they elevate a subject whose particular nature might be, nevertheless, simple and pleasant.

We shall discuss Sweetness next. The example that I cited a moment ago is even simpler because it has been broken down into a number of distinct parts, as we showed a little earlier. To break a thought down into a number of distinct parts is itself an approach that is characteristic of Simplicity, but it is not a thought. For example, in the phrase "except for harvesters and others who work for hire" (18.51), if you make it less indefinite and dwell on the details, you will make the passage simple: "except for harvesters and diggers and binders and shepherds and herdsmen." To dwell on the details in this way would produce a passage of great Simplicity.

To prove one's point by means of oaths rather than by using facts is

327 also simple and reveals Character in the thought: "I call on all the gods and goddesses who rule Attica and Pythian Apollo," etc. (18.141) or "First, Athenians, I pray to all the gods and goddesses" (18.1). There are numerous such examples in Demosthenes, and all these oaths reveal Character and are simple. The effect is the same if one binds the audience or the opponent with an oath. Oaths such as "By Zeus and the gods, do not accept" (19.78) are not maneuvers in a debate, but attempts to prove one's character and to be persuasive. But if a speaker casts a proof or some other point that is valuable to his argument in the form of an oath, that is not simple and does more than just reveal Character. That would no longer be simply an oath, but something else that has been cast into this form. It retains its original force, but also takes on some additional quality because of the way in which it is presented, such as "No, I swear it by those of your ancestors who fought at Marathon," etc. (18.208). This is a glorious example and a proof that it was customary for Athens to struggle and to take risks on behalf of the freedom of the Greeks. But it has been cast in the form of an oath. This has produced Brilliance and Grandeur, but it is not simple and does not just reveal Character. But enough about this. We must now return to our discussion. Such thoughts as these are simple.

The approaches that produce Simplicity are the same as those that 328 produce Purity, and whatever we said in our discussion of Purity could be said here as well, namely, that you can make a passage appear to be simple, even though it is not so in reality as far as the thoughts are concerned, by using other features of style such as figures and diction. For example, sharpness (*oxytēs*) or saying something pointedly (*oxeōs*), either in opposition to some speech or in some other way, which some call a kind of Subtlety (*drimytēs*),[12] or the use of striking words and turns of phrase, is not only not simple but is in fact the opposite of Simplicity. Such a style is typical of Force, since sharpness itself is nothing other than superficial profundity (*bathytēs*). Or call it Subtlety —the name makes no difference to me. As I was saying, if we introduce a straightforward thought superficially, it seems to be simple even though it might be profound. That is what often happens in Xenophon. This will become clearer a little later, when we discuss Sweetness.

The diction that is characteristic of Simplicity is for the most part the same as that which is typical of Purity. There are, however, certain

words that are peculiar to Simplicity, such as "to call brother" (*adelphizein*) in Isocrates (19.30) or "smiles mingled with tears" (*klausigelōs*) in Xenophon (*Hell.* 7.2.9) and other similar words. These reveal Character and are very simple. Striking words are also appropriate, but we shall discuss these presently in our treatment of Subtlety and sharpness, as I said before. These usually create Sweetness in Simplicity, and Sweetness is, as it were, the Beauty of Simplicity. We shall also discuss 329
this shortly. First we shall deal with Sweetness, then with Subtlety and Sharpness. But now we must return to our treatment of Simplicity. The diction peculiar to it has already been discussed.

The figures and clauses that are typical of Simplicity are the same as those that one finds in a pure style. The word order is also similar, but even more artless and loose, such as one finds in Xenophon and Aeschines the Socratic and Nicostratus: "Hear me defending myself justly" (18.6). And from what I have already said it should be obvious what the rhythm should be like in a simple passage. The word order, as usual, creates the rhythm.

The cadence or rhythmical close of a clause must be stately in a simple passage. Although this kind of cadence is typical of Solemnity, it is nevertheless more appropriate in a simple passage than a cadence that is, as it were, open and suspended. That kind of cadence is more typical of Beauty, whereas a steady rhythm and a stately cadence are characteristic of Simplicity. I have discussed these matters in my treatment of Beauty.

I promised to say something about Sweetness and grace (*hōra*), which are, as we said, intense forms of Simplicity. Therefore we shall discuss these now, and then we shall deal with Subtlety or Sharpness.

Sweetness (*Glykytēs*)   330

4 Sweet thoughts and those that give pleasure are especially ones that deal with myth: "When Aphrodite was born, the other gods and Resource, the son of Cunning, feasted," etc., which is from the *Symposium* of Plato (203b). The story about the cicadas in the *Phaedrus* is also typical: "These were once men, before the Muses were born," etc. (259b). In Demosthenes there are examples in the speech *Against Aristocrates*:

"In this court only did the gods deem it worthy to give and take justice from one another" up to "the twelve gods meted out justice to the Eumenides and Orestes" (66). But in this speech, since mythical stories are tedious and slow the pace in a practical oration, Demosthenes has used techniques that are characteristic of Rapidity and has told the story very concisely to keep it from becoming tedious. In our discussion of Force we shall deal more precisely with the approaches that should be used in telling mythical stories. But now we return to the matter at hand.

First of all, to repeat my initial point, mythical elements especially create Sweetness and give pleasure in a speech. Secondly, the narration of stories that are like myths, such as the story of the Trojan War, has the same effect. Third in order are those narrations that have some mythical quality but are more believable than myths, such as what one finds in Herodotus. A few of his stories are pure myth, such as the one about Pan (6.105) and the one about Iacchus (8.65) and perhaps a very few others. But this is not true of the others, which can be believed to have taken place and do not have a very strong mythical quality, which is why they are less sweet than those stories that are naturally mythical.

In addition to these there is another kind of thought that gives pleasure and produces Sweetness. Sometimes this has one effect, and sometimes it has another. Often it gives even more pleasure than mythical stories, but often it is less sweet than stories such as those that one finds in Herodotus. This happens as follows. The description of anything that is pleasing to our senses, to the sight or to the touch or to the taste or to any other source of sensory pleasure, this, like those ideas already discussed, produces pleasure. There are some pleasures that are shameful to enjoy, but the ones that I have mentioned are not of that sort. To describe simply those that are not shameful, such as the beauty of a place and remarkable plants and the various qualities of rivers and other such things, creates Sweetness. For they bring pleasure to the sight when they are seen and to the ear when someone describes them, as Sappho does: "Cold water rushes around through the apple branches" and "When the leaves have been shaken, their ornamentation flows away" (fr. 4). The rest of this poem is similar, as is the following passage from the *Phaedrus* of Plato: "By Hera, the resting place is beautiful. For the plane tree itself spreads wide and is high," etc. (230b). Anyone who describes these things in this way would create pleasure and Sweetness.

And pleasures that are shameful because of the source from which they are derived produce a pleasure and Sweetness to the ear corresponding to the experience itself. Whatever anyone enjoys doing he will also enjoy hearing described. A lewd man will enjoy the description of lewd acts, and a man who is self-controlled will enjoy the description of prudent acts. In fact anyone who acts in any way will enjoy the description of that kind of action. For example, the line "The son of Saturn spoke and embraced his wife in his arms" (Hom. *Il.* 14.346) produces quite a lot of pleasure, because it is modestly stated with restraint. But the style is not pleasurable. The word "he embraced" (*emarpte*) sounds rough and hard. And don't you see how the word "in his arms" (*ankas*), both because of the way it is pronounced and the way it sounds, is typical of Grandeur rather than pleasure, if you isolate it from the thought in which it appears?[13] As far as the thought is concerned, a lewd man would want to hear something more or even to describe what was done next, as in a comedy, but not a modest man. The next line, "And the divine earth grew fresh grass under them," etc. (14.347), gives more pleasure because the act described is both mythical and pleasurable by nature, because of the source of the pleasure,[14] and it was not shameful to produce such thoughts and pleasures. The following passage is similar: "And a purple wave stood about, equal to a mountain, / curved, and it hid the god and the mortal woman" (Hom. *Il.* 11.243– 244). There are thousands of such examples in the poets.

333

All amorous thoughts are usually sweet, and these occur in almost all the various kinds of Sweetness produced by the thought that we have already discussed and are, as it were, subcategories of them, which is why we have not assigned such thoughts to a separate class, but have only made mention of them.

Moreover, if anyone discusses topics that delight us, such as praises of ourselves or of our ancestors or of our children, this obviously gives pleasure. This kind of pleasure is appropriate in a political oration and often affects the audience more than those topics that are pleasurable by nature. These topics have the same effect, in fact, that we saw belonged to the report of such things as give delight to the senses.

To ascribe some rational quality to things that are irrational also produces Sweetness: "The places and the trees are not willing to teach me anything, but the men in the city are" (Pl. *Phdr.* 230d). One could argue about whether it is the style or the thought of this sentence that creates Sweetness. Perhaps it is more in the thought. For there is a trope in the phrase "are not willing," and the trope has been created by the transference of qualities from one thing to another (*metaphora*), but not as in the phrase "his speech flowed sweeter than honey" (Hom. *Il.* 1.249). In that phrase the image of "flowing" is more figurative than the idea of "being willing," which is here used more in its normal sense. Thus perhaps one would argue that to say "willing to teach me nothing" rather than "able to teach me nothing" is in effect to allegorize (*ēllēgorēsthai*). Whatever it is, this is the point that we want to make: that, generally speaking, to ascribe some moral choice to things lacking it creates Sweetness, as has been demonstrated in the preceding example. This effect is produced when Sappho questions her lyre, "Come, speak to me, divine lyre, and be eloquent," etc. (fr. 45), and the lyre responds. Herodotus gives even more examples of the phenomenon that we have been discussing. In almost the whole account of Xerxes' actions at the Hellespont he gives us pleasure by using this technique frequently: "He ordered those lashing the Hellespont to say barbarous and wicked things: 'O wicked water, your master inflicts this punishment on you because you have wronged him, although you received no injustice from him. King Xerxes will cross you, regardless of whether you want it or not. And no man will justly sacrifice to you since you are a treacherous and brackish river'" (7.35). In this passage, by portraying Xerxes as addressing the Hellespont as if it were perceptive and could make a choice, he has given tremendous pleasure, in accordance with the theory that we have just discussed. Moreover, in the poets poetic license allows this procedure. But the examples in the poets are more extreme than those that we have discussed, as in the following from the *Iliad*: "The great sky trumpeted all around" (22.388) and "Of their own free will the gates of heaven groaned open" (5.749) and "The sea stood apart in joy" (8.29). Homer speaks of the sky and the gates and the sea, not as beings that have no choice, but as able to know what must be done. Such procedures are allowed to poets. But here too it is the sentiments in such passages that produce Sweetness and give pleasure, although less than in the others that we discussed.

The same thing also happens if you attribute human qualities to dumb beasts, as Xenophon does when he says that dogs frown and smile and trust or distrust tracks (*Cyn.* 3.5, 4.3, 3.7) and when he says: "But being confident they do not allow their wise fellow workers to advance, but prevent them by barking" (3.7). Terms like "fellow workers" and "wise" apply to men, not to dogs. In fact that is true of everything that is said in this passage. You could find many similar examples in the *Cynegeticus*, in which the thought naturally gives much pleasure. Indeed it is so, in several ways, but especially in reference to the thought, because the activity of hunting is naturally pleasing to the sight, as Xenophon himself points out when he says that there is no more pleasurable spectacle than to see a hare roused, fleeing, pursued, and taken. But this is enough about the thoughts that produce Sweetness and pleasure. The approaches that create Sweetness are the same as those that produce Purity and Simplicity, which we have already discussed.

The style that produces Sweetness is the same as the one that is char-   336
acteristic of Simplicity, which is similar to the pure style, and one that is poetical. Herodotus, who was particularly concerned with Sweetness, therefore used both the approaches that produce it and the thoughts that, in our opinion, are characteristic of it, and each style that is peculiar to Simplicity, as we have already said. One reason the Sweetness in his work is so remarkable is that he chose to use a dialect that is poetical. The Ionic dialect, since it is associated with poetry, naturally gives a lot of pleasure. It doesn't really matter whether he also uses some words from other dialects, since Homer and Hesiod and quite a few other poets do the same thing. But they generally use Ionic. And Ionic, as I said, has a poetic flavor, and because of that it is pleasing.

I think that for the same reason poetic references and reminiscences in a passage also give pleasure: " 'We two, going together,' will discuss what we will say" (Pl. *Symp.* 174d; Hom. *Il.* 10.224). In the fifth book of the *Republic* we have the same phenomenon: "But also in Homer we see that it is just to honor such young men as are noble. Indeed Homer says that Ajax, who was distinguished in the war, 'was honored with whole chines,' since this was a suitable reward for a young and courageous man, from which he would derive honor and increase his   337
strength" (5.468c–d; *Il.* 7.321) and "Shall we not believe Hesiod, who says that when people of this race die, 'They become holy spirits who

dwell on earth, / Good and watchful guardians of mortal men?' We shall surely believe him" (5.468e; *Op.* 122–123). There are also many such passages in Xenophon and quite a few other authors, and there is an abundance of examples if anyone would be willing to cull them from each author.

In the *Symposium* Plato has Agathon, since he was a poet, frequently lace his language with references to poetry. He does not use references from the poems of others but quotes his own poetry. However, he gives notice that he will quote poetry, so that the quotation does not appear to pop up from nowhere. He says, for example: "I am moved to quote some poetry and to say that Eros is the one who makes"—then he quotes the verses—"'Peace among men, and calm on the sea, / and repose for the winds, and rest and sleep in our pain'" (197c). Likewise, in the *Phaedrus*, Socrates, taking the role of someone else, or at least pretending that someone else is speaking since he is under divine inspiration, quotes a verse: "'As wolves love a lamb, so lovers love their beloved'" (241d). Even this is not allowed to pass without an apology of sorts; here too he introduces a corrective.[15] Moreover, you must realize that whether you are quoting your own poetry or someone else's, the references must be woven into the passage in such a way that the quotations from poetry and the prose seem to form one body rather than distinct entities, as when laws and decrees are read out during speeches. For that produces something other than real Sweetness, as in: "Read to me also the verses that you butchered, 'I come from the dwelling of the dead and the gates of gloom' and 'Know that I announce sad tidings against my will'" (Dem. 18.267). The same is true of the quotation from Sophocles' *Antigone* in the speech *On the False Embassy*: "'It is impossible to know the temper of any man,'" etc. (247; *Ant.* 175). Perhaps someone would say that there is an element of Sweetness in these passages, even if it is slight. But, as I said, it is obvious to me that if there is a clear distinction between the poetic references and the prose passage in which they are quoted, either the pleasure-producing quality of the reference will be lost or it will be weakened considerably.

We must now return to our discussion of the style that produces Sweetness. A sweet style is also one that uses epithets: "Come now, clear-voiced Muses" (Pl. *Phdr.* 237a). In poetry, which is naturally sweet in comparison with prose, epithets seem to be even sweeter in

338

some way and to give even more pleasure (*hēdonē*). The poetry of
Stesichorus seems to be very sweet because he uses a lot of epithets. 339
And the subtle style [which involves the use of striking words and turns
of phrase] is also one that produces Sweetness. We shall discuss that
next.

The figures that produce Sweetness are the same as those that we said
were characteristic of Simplicity and Purity. Those that produce Beauty
and a finely wrought passage are also appropriate.

The word order that creates Sweetness is the same as that which
produces Beauty, obviously one that makes the passage almost metrical,
for in the ordering of the words a sweet passage must give some pleasure
to the ear. Moreover, the metrical feet that are characteristic of Solemnity should be used primarily. The cadences in a passage that gives
pleasure should be solemn and stately, for the rhythm must be so, as we
pointed out to be the case with Simplicity as well.

Subtlety (*Drimytēs*) and Speaking Pointedly (*Oxeōs Legein*) and a Speech That Is Graceful (*Hōraios*) and Pretty (*Habros*) and Pleasurable (*Hēdonēn Exontos*)

5 I promised that I would say something about Subtlety (*drimytēs*)
and sharpness (*oxytēs*), since they are appropriate to a passage that is
simple and gives pleasure. We mentioned a little earlier, in our discussion of Simplicity, what kinds of thoughts are typical of this style and
pointed out that they are those that are, as it were, superficially profound. But perhaps not to express cunningly contrived thoughts in a
clever way, but to express them simply and directly, is not really a
thought but rather an approach. That is why this is an approach that is
typical of Simplicity. I said that there are many examples of this in
Xenophon, which one would expect because his style is simple.

There is another kind of Subtlety or sharpness in addition to the one 340
that we have already discussed. It is hard to explain whether this kind
involves a question of the diction or of the thought. One cannot say
with certainty either that it is a thought or that it is not. It is seen in
reference to the diction, but the diction that creates Subtlety, in and of
itself, has no element of Subtlety if it is separated from the thought that

it expresses or from the preceding context of that thought. In the other types that is not possible. A pure diction, for example, remains pure, even if someone uses it to express a solemn thought and nothing has been said previously. A solemn diction remains solemn, even if one should use it to express a thought that is not solemn and there is no context. The same is true of the other types. But the diction that is characteristic of Subtlety is not like this. It has no subtle quality in and of itself, but is used to express some thought in an unusual way, or it becomes subtle by attaching some witty or ironic comment to what precedes and thus creates Subtlety. Examples will make this clearer. A word can be used to express a thought with which it is not usually associated. Xenophon, for example, when he is discussing why hunting dogs return from their pursuit before they should (*Cyn.* 3.8), says that some do this out of laziness, and some out of lack of experience, and some for other reasons, and some out of "philanthropy." In this passage he has called the dogs' relationship with men and their pleasure in asso-

341 ciating with men "philanthropy," although the word is not properly used in that way (for we are accustomed to conceive of "philanthropy" in another way), although in an etymological sense ("a love of men") the word does describe the relationship that Xenophon has in mind. In fact, from an etymological point of view, the word is probably used more properly in this passage from Xenophon than it is to express pity for others and compassion, which is the way in which the word is usually used. Another example comes from Sophocles (fr. 1006). He says that Atalanta was a "philanderer" ("a lover of men") because she liked to be around men, although we generally think of this word as meaning something else, as is the case with "philanthropy." There is another example in Euripides: "Woman, do not surpass your mother in philandery" (*Andr.* 229). In these passages the word "philanderer" or "philandery" has a meaning that is almost opposite to the way in which we are accustomed to use it. Now it usually means licentiousness and adultery. People also speak of a "well-minded" word when they mean one that is easily understood and clear. And Euphorion says: "the people of the Athenians, who show no fear" (fr. 159) instead of saying that the Athenians are not afraid and are fearless.[16] In general, however, in using words subtly one must be very careful not to lapse into frigidity or bad taste (*psychrotēs*). For those who combine the serious and the comic for the sake of a laugh are praised in fact because they use such clever

expressions. Thus one must be cautious. This is the first kind of Subtlety
of which there is no example in Demosthenes.   342

There are three other kinds of Subtlety that Demosthenes does use.
All are produced by using some word in conjunction with its preceding
context, but they are different from one another. The use of words that
sound similar, for example, creates a certain amount of Subtlety "He is
going (*mellei*) to besiege the Greeks, he betrays them. For is anyone
concerned (*melei*) about the Asiatic Greeks?" (8.27). I was very hesitant
to quote this as an example of Subtlety. Some who were very famous in
a previous generation and are now admired because of their theory of
oratory have taken this view in the books that they have left behind
them, and have quoted this as an example of this kind of Subtlety. Let
us therefore record their view. Perhaps not even this sort of Subtlety, if
it were produced in this way, escapes the charge of frigidity. Yet let the
case be put. And, as we said, this effect is created through the use of two
words that sound alike.

There is another kind of Subtlety that consists in the use of a word
first in its proper sense and then in a figurative way (*paronomasia*),
rather than by using words that sound alike. This happens when you
use a noun or a verb in its usual sense and then use it in an unusual
way: "Unless you will say that those who set up engines of war are
moving for (*agein*) peace until they move (*agein*) these up against the
walls" (9.17). Then Demosthenes says why he thinks that Philip is at   343
war with Athens and that everything that Philip is now doing and preparing is being prepared against the Athenians. Then he uses a sentence
that is subtle: "Then am I to say that the one who has set up this engine
of war against the city is moving for (*agein*) peace? Absolutely not"
(9.18). There is another example: "I do not fear whether Philip is alive
or has died, but whether the spirit in our city that hates and punishes
those who do wrong has died" (19.289). This not only makes the passage subtle but also gives it vividness (*enargēs*). This is almost a metaphor (*tropē*), but not exactly, because it simply involves the use of a
word in an unusual way. If you should say "the spirit in our city that
hates wrongdoers has died" out of this context, the trope would sound
very stiff. But used in conjunction with another sentence to create word-
play it makes the passage vivid and subtle.

The third kind of Subtlety is the only one left, and Demosthenes uses
that as well. This is created when a writer uses a trope that is not very

strong or harsh and then introduces one that is stronger, but does not seem to be so because it follows the one that has already been used: "Such things endure once and for a brief season, and indeed, encouraged by hopes, they blossom perhaps, but in time they are detected and fall to pieces" (2.10). The image of "blossoming" is metaphorical, but it

344 is not strong or stiff. But to say "they fall to pieces" is very unusual and sounds strange, although less so here because it follows the first image. One could properly say of withering flowers that they fall apart, but the phrase that is used in conjunction with this image, "in time they are detected," has diluted it considerably. There is a similar example in the *Polyidos* of Euripides: "For if the bird that dwells upon the waves / Had flown from land to sea, it would have told / 'The child has died among the watery waves'" (fr. 636 N.[2]). Here "it would have told" is next to "dwells upon," but by itself it would have somehow been harsh. But this is enough about Subtlety and sharpness, both of which are appropriate in Simplicity and Sweetness.

Our whole treatment of pleasure and Sweetness applies as well to prettiness and the so-called graceful style and others that are similar. As far as I am concerned all these differ in name only and are really the same. For whenever we express some amorous thought or any of the others that are characteristic of Sweetness or use such an approach and express ourselves by means of epithets and poetic words and use balanced phrases and clauses or some other figure that is typical of Beauty and order the words in the sentence in such a way as to create rhythms that are solemn and beautiful and use cadences that are characteristic of Solemnity and Simplicity, our style necessarily becomes graceful and pretty. So I am not sure whether there is any difference at all

345 between pleasure and the charm that one finds in a passage that exemplifies prettiness or Sweetness or any other such style. But here I bring to a close my treatment of Simplicity and Sweetness. Next we shall discuss Modesty.

Modesty (*Epieikeia*)

6 A passage that reveals a modest character is produced mainly by the thought and is created whenever anyone states that of his own free will he is aiming at less than he could attain, as Demosthenes does in the

speech *Against Conon* (1.24) when he declares that although he could bring a charge of theft or violence, he is nevertheless content to make an accusation for assault. The same effect is produced whenever anyone equates himself with the average man although that is not really true, and this produces almost the same impression as the procedure mentioned first. For generally speaking Modesty is, as Plato says (*Leg.* 6.757e), a violation of justice, which should give every man his due, perpetrated out of a love for humanity. To count yourself among the common people when you are not of that rank is nothing other than willingly to aim at less than you could attain. Nevertheless we shall consider them to be two different kinds of Modesty, equating yourself with the common crowd being the second kind. Demosthenes often uses this procedure in the speech *Against Meidias*. In fact in the opening of the speech he says: "I myself did what each one of you would have chosen to do if you had been insulted" (1). Whether this is also forceful is another question. To know how to use the various kinds of style suitably, as well as the other features of oratory, is by nature characteristic of Force, and in this passage Demosthenes has appropriately used Modesty and the revelation of Character (*ēthos*), since it is modest to grant some point to one's opponent willingly. Consider how forcefully Demosthenes does this. In the speech *Against Aristocrates* he concedes 346 that Charidemus should be treated as a citizen, so that he can more easily prove that the decree in question is illegal.[17] For normal legal procedures apply in the case of citizens [who have been murdered]. Consider how he calls attention to his Modesty in the following passage from this speech: "Observe," he says, "how reasonably and simply I will construct my argument, since I place him in the same rank in which he would attain the greatest respect," etc. (24).

It is also indicative of Modesty to say that you are going to trial against your will and that you have come to court only because you have been compelled to do so by your opponent, whereas the matter should have been settled among friends and relatives. "If Aphobus were willing to do what is just," etc. (27.1) produces an impression of Modesty, as do the following passages: "Although I have not brought a suit against any citizen or criticized anyone's accounts," etc. (Aeschin. 1.1) or "Although I am not involved in politics nor am I one of those who come into court often, I say that I shall demonstrate that such a crime was perpetrated," etc. (Dem. 23.4).

To assert that you have come into court although you are unaccustomed to public speaking disarms the jury and reveals Modesty and your general character by arguing that you speak only when you are compelled to do so. At the same time you show that you have come to court against your will. Generally speaking, as I argued at the beginning of this discussion, any statement that gives the impression that a person willingly aims at less than he could attain reveals a modest character.

347   Whenever someone is being prosecuted, he can use all the techniques just discussed by turning the tables on his opponent. He can argue, for example, that he is being prosecuted although he himself could have prosecuted his opponent and that his opponent feels contempt for him because he is a good citizen and a man of the common people and that he himself has never brought a charge against anyone and has even now come into court unwillingly. In other words, as I said, the defendant can use all the procedures described above. There are many examples of such techniques in the private speeches of Demosthenes and even more in Lysias and Hyperides. For these orators were naturally more concerned with character portrayal, especially in the approaches that they use.

The first approach that is characteristic of Modesty is very similar to modest thoughts, and involves giving up some of your own advantages or toning down arguments that are strongest against your opponent and not delivering them as vehemently as you could. Demosthenes sometimes willingly uses an approach that plays down his own accomplishments. He can also speak grandiloquently, as he does when he says, "After this I sent out all the expeditions in which the Chersonese was saved and Byzantium and all our allies" (18.80). But elsewhere in the same speech he says, "I do claim some credit for having administered particular measures" (18.206). Do you see how the same activity is referred to in both passages, namely, that he gave advice and made proposals, but how much more modest and humble the latter is? He uses

348   both passages appropriately, not in Modesty but with Force [because he knew what tone was suitable in the various parts of his speech]. Thus he plays down his accomplishments in the latter passage and plays them up in the former.

Anyone who wants to produce a passage that reveals a modest character would, in my opinion, use the approach exemplified by the second of the two passages from Demosthenes quoted above, but there are few examples of such an approach. Hence I was not able on the spur of the moment to come up with another example of an approach of this sort from Demosthenes or any other writer. Ironic passages, which involve mock modesty and ignorance purposely affected, are not modest. Such passages do reveal Character, but they are indignant rather than modest: "Perhaps it is foolishness to do something beyond one's power" (21.69) or "You want me, whom you would derisively and slanderously call Batalus" (18.180) and many other examples. These passages are indignant, and because of that they reveal Character, but they are not modest nor do they reveal a modest Character. Thus, as I said, there are few examples of such an approach, and consequently I have not been able to provide you with others "since another task calls me" (Hom. *Od.* 11.54), as the poet truly says. But I think that I have been able to indicate clearly the nature of Modesty, so that anyone who looks carefully would, perhaps without difficulty, find suitable examples of this. There would be quite a few in Plato, in those passages in which Socrates has something to say about himself. And I think that there is a passage of this sort in the *Charmides* (175a) and in the *Symposium* (222c), after the speeches of Alcibiades. There are many others elsewhere.

349

In any case you could play down your own advantages by using a modest passage that relies upon the sort of approach that I have described. There are two [further] approaches that can be used to soften what normally would be said with Vehemence against your opponent. You can do this either by indicating that you have chosen to speak moderately, or you can simply do so without calling attention to what you are doing. When you indicate what you are doing, the passage has a certain vehement quality, slight, but nevertheless there: "Do not be angry with me, for I will not say anything base against you" (20.102) or "In other respects I do not know the intention of the one who proposed the law, and I do not say anything base about him nor am I aware of anything of that sort, but judging from the law itself I find that it is very different from him," etc. (20.13). When you do not indicate what you are doing, the passage becomes completely modest because of that: "Why, then, if not some, but all, were unworthy in most respects, did he consider you and them worthy of the same treatment?" (20.2). You see how he could have expressed this vehemently if he had wanted to: "Why, if not some, but all, were unworthy in most respects, did he condemn you and them to the same dishonor? For he strips them of their immunity, and takes from you the power to grant an immunity to whomever you wish." He has expressed himself in a way that reveals a very modest character by saying "he considered you and them *worthy of the same treatment.*" There is a similar example in the deliberative

350 speeches: "The Spartans seem to me to be doing the work of dangerous men" (16.16).[18] To hesitate and not to declare openly that the Spartans are dangerous, but to say "they seem to me," or rather not even to say that they seem to be dangerous but that they are similar to dangerous men and to be undertaking some task that is typical of dangerous men, is characteristic of a man who has shunned an impetuous and vehement style and uses one that reveals a modest character. This is clear if we look at the speeches against Philip, since there Demosthenes expresses himself in a way that is opposite to the type now under discussion: "Being a man who is unscrupulous and dangerous" (1.3). First, he uses the word "unscrupulous" and not simply "dangerous." "Unscrupulous" is certainly a stronger word than "dangerous." Moreover, he does not say that Philip *seems* to him to be unscrupulous nor does he hesitate or show any doubt, as he did in the passage cited earlier, but he states it openly and directly. In addition, he does not say, as he did of the Spartans, that Philip is *like* unscrupulous or dangerous men, but that he *is* in fact unscrupulous and dangerous. Thus this passage is vehement and harsh, whereas the other reveals a modest character and a speaker who has shunned Vehemence. You could find quite a few examples of such an approach, whereby a speaker softens what is said against his opponents, as Demosthenes does in the deliberative speeches and in the speech *Against Leptines* (here I am not talking about the first technique discussed above, whereby someone could play down his own advantages). Even if the speech *Against Leptines* is contentious in tone, nevertheless it reveals Character when Demosthenes discusses the people involved, as well as in the approach used and possibly in other respects, as in the deliberative speeches.

But we must return to our discussion. The first approach that is char-
351 acteristic of Modesty is the one just outlined. The second is one that uses the figure in which a fact is passed over on purpose (*paraleipsis*). To choose to omit some point that you could say against your opponent or on your own behalf seems to be indicative of a modest character. Such omissions add much credibility because of the impression of Modesty that they produce. This effect can be created in two ways, as I said, by

passing over either arguments that are used against us or those that can be used on our behalf. And there are two kinds, as we pointed out was the case in softening attacks on our opponent. First of all, you can omit something outright, or you can mention it but not develop the thought, indicating only that some basically undefined argument has been omitted: "I shall pass over those speeches concerning which there is some dispute whether they were delivered in the city's best interests" (18.131) or "I shall pass over many things for one reason," he says, "or another" (cf. 10.10, 18.258). This is the first kind of *paraleipsis*. In the second kind you only use an approach that indicates an omission, but then you narrate the facts that you promised to omit: "I would not mention that I have ransomed some citizens from our enemies and have given dowries to some girls from poor families" (18.268) or "I pass over Olynthus and Methone and thirty-two cities in Thrace," etc. (9.26). Of these two kinds of omissions, the one that narrates the fact, such as I just cited, creates trustworthiness and reveals Character. The other, the one that does not discuss what is in question, such as "I shall pass over those speeches concerning which there is some dispute whether they were delivered in the city's best interests," creates trustworthiness and reveals Character and also produces Abundance, since some undefined   352 argument is being added. Such passages simply add an undefined idea or something else indefinite that is introduced by means of a *paraleipsis*.

The third approach that is typical of Modesty is the one that produces a pure passage, which is the same as the one that creates Simplicity. One who wants to appear to be modest must speak in a style that gives the impression of being very simple, the sort of style that someone who is quite unskilled in the rules of rhetoric would understand.

The diction of a modest passage is the same as that which produces Purity and Simplicity, and this is true of the figures, the clauses, the word order, the cadences, and the rhythms as well, if these features of style can contribute anything to producing a passage that appears to be modest.

Sincere Style (*Alēthinos Logos*)

7 An unaffected and sincere and, as it were, animated style is primarily produced by the approach and the figures and the diction and

whatever other elements are related to these, but the thought is also important. All simple thoughts would usually be appropriate in an unaffected style. Otherwise how could they really be simple? Perhaps modest thoughts are also of this kind. But more than these, angry complaints are typical of the animated style: "Being himself, I think, a marvelous soldier, by Zeus" (19.113). After the indignation that is produced by the irony of this passage, he adds "by Zeus." This expression adds another element of anger to what has already been said. The following is similar: "But Androtion is the one who repairs the vessels that you use in solemn processions: Androtion—O Earth and Gods!" (22.78). Perhaps this involves a question of the approach rather than of the thought. But the passage "Are you deliberating whether Charidemus deserves personal protection? Charidemus? Alas!" (23.210) has a characteristic thought in the word "alas." You could find thousands of examples of this in Demosthenes.

The thoughts that are characteristic of an unaffected passage are, in my opinion, familiar and clearly to be seen. If an approach that expresses anger is used with a thought that is not by nature emotional (e.g., not naturally connected with anger), as in the example "But Androtion is the one who repairs the vessels that you use in solemn processions: Androtion—O Earth and Gods!" the approach is certainly obvious and is not difficult to understand.

The other approaches that are characteristic of a sincere passage are almost impossible to describe. Whether you use prayers or some similar appeal, it is not simply because of these prayers or appeals that the passage becomes unaffected and spontaneous, but these are aspects of Simplicity that reveal Character. There are other features in addition to these that, in my opinion, make a passage seem to be animated. For example, "First of all, Athenians, I pray to all the gods and goddesses" (18.1) is, to be sure, a prayer, but it is similar in a way to "Would that we were at this stage of alarm!" which is spoken by Aristides in the *Sicilians*.[19] I do not mean that this is better than what Demosthenes says—I would be a madman if I said that—but that the passage by Aristides is more sincere than the one in Demosthenes. The occasion did not require that Demosthenes straightway, at the outset of his speech, use a style that in some way reveals Sincerity, but rather one that reveals his character more generally. We demonstrated this and many other related points in our discussion of the speech *On the Crown*.[20] You could also find quite a few examples of passages that reveal Sincerity in Demosthenes. "I call upon all the gods and goddesses who protect the land of Attica and Pythian Apollo," etc. (18.141) is obviously an oath. But consider whether it is similar to the following passage: "Unless it was only out of a desire to rescue those men, may I utterly perish from the face of the earth if any amount of money would have persuaded me to go on an embassy with these men" (19.172). Here, moreover, the use of a simple style throughout the sentence has made the phrase "any amount" even more unaffected and spontaneous.

We must return to our original point that the approaches that produce an unaffected and spontaneous style are almost indescribable. Nevertheless we must be bold enough to discuss them and attempt to describe them if we are able. Now I say that there is one approach that is typical of almost every spontaneous passage, and that is not to give any advance indication that you will use an oath or a prayer but simply to slip into it naturally, as it were, as Demosthenes does in the phrase "would that I were not acquainted with him now" in the following passage: "When I brought suit against my guardians, when I was a mere boy and neither knew this man nor whether he existed—would that I were not acquainted with him now" (21.78). To express amazement over a certain situation also reveals a spontaneous Character. But if you indicate your amazement in advance, this lessens the spontaneous nature of the passage. It would still reveal Character and perhaps would be simple and in this respect it would have some element of Sincerity, although this would be clouded. But if you omit any advance notice that you are amazed at something and simply recite what amazes you in such a way that your amazement is obvious, you will make the passage more spontaneous and truly animated: "Although he is well aware of how he has lived his life, this filthy scoundrel will dare to look you in the eye and with his sonorous voice will discourse upon how he has lived, which makes me choke with rage. Don't these men know you?" etc. (19.199). The phrases "which makes me choke with rage. Don't these men know you?" are vehement and create a very spontaneous tone, since the speaker is amazed that his opponent dares to say such things. And consider the following passage: "Are you deliberating, Athenians, although the Thebans are on the island, about what you should do? Will

355

you not be aroused?" etc. (8.74). Simply put, as I said in the preceding discussion, this is one approach that can be used in a passage that is really going to appear to be animated: not to indicate in advance that you have any emotion in your heart, either amazement or fear or anger 356 or grief or pity or confidence or disbelief or irritation or any such emotion, but to introduce the point in such a way that you thus reveal the emotion that you feel, either anger or amazement or whatever else, as the occasion demands. The following show anger: "Then, you wretched scribbler" (18.209) and "Although he is well aware of how he has lived his life, this filthy scoundrel" (19.199) and other such examples. Demosthenes shows pity when he speaks of the "miserable Phocians" (19.128) and when he says, "But the miserable man has been dishonored and insulted" (19.284). An example of amazement is "Do I reproach you for your friendship with Alexander?" etc. (18.51) or the passage cited earlier: "Are you deliberating, Athenians, although the Thebans are on the island, about what you should do?" Perhaps there is not in the orators any passage that shows fear, but there are thousands of examples in the comedians and in the tragedians. The passages already cited, "Charidemus? Alas!" and "Androtion—O Earth and Gods!" show irritation. The following shows confidence: "I am ready to sail out as a volunteer and suffer any consequence if this is not true" (4.29). Likewise, to use rapid replies to objections, especially when the objections and the replies are not formally introduced (*chōris katastaseōs*),[21] is typical of a spontaneous passage that is delivered with confidence. Demosthenes asks, for example: "Where indeed shall we land, someone has asked?" Then he gives the reply without a formal introduction: "The war itself, Athenians, will find his weak spots" (4.44). Similar is the following: "Are the Byzantines wretches? Of course. But nevertheless they must be saved. 357 For that is beneficial to Athens" (8.16). This approach is also typical of Rapidity. I said already, in my discussion of Rapidity, that I would treat provisional concurrence with an adversary's argument (*syndromē*)—or should we call it concession (*synchōrēsis*)?—more fully when I deal with the approach that is characteristic of Force. It would be more appropriate to discuss it there.

We must return to our discussion. In general, to make a basic point without a formal introduction and without using connectives is spontaneous and sincere: "By Zeus, we should have done this, but we should not have done that" (9.68). Then Demosthenes uses a parenthesis that is not formally introduced and does not use connectives, which is very spontaneous: "The Olynthians would be able to say many things now, which, if they had known them then, they would not have been destroyed, likewise with the Phocians, likewise with all those who have been destroyed." The passage that follows this one is similar: "But what use are these things now?" (69). Then, again without a connective or preparation, he says very spontaneously: "While the ship is safe, the sailor and the pilot and every man on board must be zealous; but when the sea is high, zeal is in vain."[22] Perhaps someone would argue that this is a figure and not an approach, but that is not the case. It is not simply the use of no connective that makes this passage spontaneous but also the fact that there is no formal presentation and that this is an answer to an objection. Replies are not figures but approaches of sorts, or at any rate thoughts.

There is another approach in addition to those already discussed that is typical of a spontaneous passage, especially one that seems to be spoken in anger, and that is not to preserve the natural sequence of the thought but to seem to lose control because of emotion: "Since, therefore, the vote has seemed righteous and just to all—but I must, as it seems, although I am not a slanderer," etc. (18.126) up to "and although I am not at a loss as to what I should say about you and your family, I am at a loss about where I should begin" (129). Nowhere in this sentence does Demosthenes follow the sequence that one would expect; his emotion has disturbed, as it were, the natural order of the sentence. This makes the passage seem to be even more spontaneous and truthful. And it is clear from another passage in the same section of this speech that to use abusive language without giving any advance notice that you are going to do so is characteristic of a truthful and spontaneous passage: "If Aeacus or Rhadamanthus or Minos were my accuser, rather than a scandalmonger, a loafer from the marketplace, a wretched scribe" (18.127). This too, in my opinion, is an approach, whereby the one who uses abusive language does not seem to give offense because he shows clearly, by the very fact that he does not give any advance indication of what he will do, that he has been carried away by anger and has not thought out in advance the abusive comments that he makes about his opponent before he came into court, but has said things against his

358

opponent that occurred to him on the spur of the moment and were dictated by anger. The use of such approaches makes the passage more persuasive because of the orator's emotional state and because the insults have been delivered in an emphatic and spontaneous way. But if you give an advance indication of what you are doing, as Aeschines does when he says, "'Give me the right to call him a lewd fellow'" (cf. Aeschin. 2.88), you will not be as persuasive and you will appear to be someone who enjoys slander. One who has really suffered and is moved and is overcome by emotion and does not know what he is saying does not give an advance indication of what he will do. To do so indicates a person who is sober and knows what he is doing and has planned this out and who desires to slander his opponent. We do not believe this kind of person, because he does not speak spontaneously or vividly. Someone who speaks spontaneously seems to be very convinced of what he is saying, but someone who seems to have planned out his remarks is not equally convincing.

There is another approach that is typical of a sincere and, as it were, animated passage. It is almost the same as the one just described, but with a slight difference. This is the technique of seeming to say something that occurs to you on the spur of the moment rather than something that was thought out in advance, not only when you use abusive language, but also elsewhere: "Indeed this point almost escaped me" (cf. 21.110) and "Indeed I have gone into arguments that it will be more appropriate to use later" (18.42). There are many examples of this approach in Demosthenes. But this is enough about the thoughts and approaches that are typical of a spontaneous style.

Rough and vehement diction and coined words are indicative of anger, especially in sudden attacks on your opponent, where unusual words that seem to be coined on the spur of the moment are quite suitable, words such as "iamb-eater" (18.139) or "pen-pusher" (18.209). All such words are suitable since they seem to have been dictated by emotion. In sudden attacks, as I said, rough and vehement diction is effective and makes the passage sound true and gives it vigor. This kind of diction, however, is not always useful when we want to give indication of some other emotion. It would be very out of place, for example, in a passage whose purpose is to arouse pity, where Purity and Simplicity and Sweetness and pleasure would be much more appropriate.

Those styles are closely connected with pity, as Xenophon has demonstrated in the story of Abradates and Pantheia (*Cyr.* 7.3), where he says, among other things, "the dead man's hand came off" (8). By describing an irrational thing as one would describe a rational being, he has created pleasure while increasing the pity that the passage arouses. I have often pointed out that we must deal with the question where, and in reference to what topics, the various kinds of styles are appropriate in our treatment of the approach that is characteristic of Force, where we shall discuss these questions fully.

The figures that are characteristic of a passage that is animated by an attack on one's opponent are the same as those that produce Vehemence: that is, direct addresses, such as "They stayed with you, Aeschines, and you sponsored them" (18.82), and direct addresses used in conjunction with a question, which are more animated mainly because of the tone of cross-examination that they display: "Why in the world, Eubulus, at the trial of Hegesilaus, who is your cousin, and recently at the one of Thrasybulus, who is the uncle of Niceratus?" etc. (19.290). There are innumerable examples of this figure. The passage "Are you similar, Aeschines? Is your brother? Are any of the orators today?" etc. (18.318), however, is indignant because of the irony, though it does have an animated quality because of the figure of speech. On the whole the passage reveals Character, since Indignation has been combined with the spontaneous in the approach that is used to introduce the thought. Another figure that is spontaneous is a "pointing" expression (*deiktikon*), which is also vehement, such as "*This* is the man who now laments the misfortunes of the Thebans" (18.41).

361

Doubting or perplexity (*diaporēsis*) has the same effect: "Then, o— What can one call you to give you the right name?" (18.22). This conveys spontaneity because Demosthenes does not give any advance indication that he is perplexed, but shows what emotion he feels by the style itself, as we pointed out in our discussion of the approach that is characteristic of this type. This is either a figure or an approach, as we said, but we have chosen to discuss it with the figures that convey spontaneity or animation.

Breaking off a sentence abruptly (*aposiōpēsis*) is also typical of a spontaneous and animated passage. The following are examples of this: "However, to me— But I do not want to say anything harsh at the very outset of my speech" (18.3) and, in the speech *For the Megalopolitans*, "It is not concerning these matters— But I will pass over what it occurred to me to say" (18).

Judgments (*epikriseis*) also have the same effect, such as "How could it be so? Far from it" (18.47). Elsewhere, having uttered an indignant complaint, Demosthenes augments the spontaneity of the passage by adding a judgment: "It is awful, O Earth and Gods—for how is it not? —to act against the best interests of one's country" (18.139). Hesitant judgments are less spontaneous, although they reveal Character and are more suitable to Indignation: "Since I am going, as it seems, to give an account today of my whole life," etc. (18.8). What I mean here will become clear in my discussion of Indignation. Perhaps a judgment should not be considered a figure but a thought, but at least we have described what effect it produces.

A correction of a previous statement (*epidiorthōsis*) that is added for the sake of amplification (*auxēsis*) also conveys spontaneity: "For recently— Do I say recently? Indeed, yesterday or the day before" (18.130) and "It is a shameful thing, or rather among the most shameful" (2.2).

The so-called unfinished or incomplete division (*apolytos merismos*) is another figure expressing spontaneity that one finds often in Demosthenes. This is almost the same as the expression of a judgment,[23] as in the following example: "If in respect to those matters in which you were honored one of you committed an injustice, and such an injustice as this, by how much more would you be hated justly, rather than delivered, because of that?" (19.238). Then there is the first half of an incomplete division, which is nothing other than an expression of opinion or a judgment: "That, on the one hand, is my view." He does not pick up the second half of the division [i.e., "on the other hand"] but immediately introduces the sentence "Therefore, perhaps, being loud and shameless, they will press hard," etc. (19.238). There are many examples of this in Demosthenes. They are used in reference to facts that are naturally agreed to or that have been proved, or that seem to be generally agreed upon or to have been proved. Because of this impression they reveal Character as well as making the passage appear to be spontaneous. The proemium of the speech *Against Timocrates* is similar: "On the one hand, gentlemen of the jury, I do not think that Timocrates himself would say that anyone else is responsible for the present trial," etc. (1), including the rest of the proemium. Here too the responding clause has not been given.[24] This passage has caused innumerable problems for those foolish scholars who claim to have explained Demosthenes and have even dared to leave behind books containing their interpretations. Many teachers even today who read those books think that they are knowledgeable and convince their students. But, as the saying goes, this is the blind leading the blind. How can they argue that Demosthenes has stated as something generally agreed upon that Timocrates has caused this trial for himself and that Diodorus, who indicted him, did not come into court out of personal animosity, because he wanted, in fact, to prove this very point? No, here Demosthenes has done, by means of an incomplete division, what he is often accustomed to do in his proemia, and that is to introduce as an obvious assumption the issue that is being investigated. This figure is often found even in the so-called common usage, and that is why it is appropriate in practical oratory: "On account of this, not even he himself would deny" (cf. 20.8). These are the figures that create a spontaneous style.

The clauses and the word order and the cadence and the rhythm that result from these and every other similar aspect of style are like those that were typical of Asperity, except when you want to produce a passage that arouses pity. Then a simpler style would be more appropriate, and you must then follow the rules laid down for Simplicity. We shall discuss these questions more fully, as we have often promised, in our treatment of the approach that is characteristic of Force.

Indignation (*Barytēs*)

364

8 Indignation is found in all reproachful thoughts whenever the speaker who is discussing his own benefactions says by way of criticism that he has received little or no gratitude for them, or, the opposite, when he says that he has in fact been thought worthy of punishment rather than honor. A passage becomes especially indignant if the speaker brings up those who have done little or no good or in fact have done wrong, but have received those honors of which he himself was not thought worthy. This is tantamount to saying, "You considered so and so, who is a bad man, worthy of these honors, but me, although I have chosen a different course, you thought worthy of the opposite." There are many examples of such thoughts in Demosthenes' letter *On Behalf of the Children of Lycurgus* and in the letter *Concerning His Own Restoration.*[25] At the very outset of the latter you find this kind of thought in the proemium: "I used to think that because of my accomplishments in politics I would surely not suffer such things, since I have never wronged you in any way," etc. (2.1).

Indignant thoughts are created even out of those that seem to be modest, whenever they are approached in such a way that the speaker willingly gives up some of his own advantages or agrees to yield an advantage to his opponent or, from what he says in his speech, obviously deems himself or his opponent worthy of deeds or words that are the opposite of those stated. Ironic statements are like this, and they clearly involve the use of a certain approach: "Perhaps someone wants to think me mad. For it is probably madness to attempt something beyond one's means" (21.69). In this passage he has created Indignation by calling his ambition madness. The following is similar: "What is your position because of these worthy men?" (3.27). We have many such examples. Every one of them is primarily, as I said, a question of the approach. For ironic statements involve a certain approach, which is what creates the Indignation in the passage. But the thought in and of itself does not exhibit any element of Indignation. Ironic statements create Indignation, as I said, because the speaker who uses irony employs an approach that indicates the opposite of what he means: "At that time, therefore, I, Batalus of the deme of Paeania, plainly deserved better of his country than you, Oenomaus of Cothocidae" (18.180).[26] By using both these names, Batalus and Oenomaus, he indicates ideas that are opposite to the words themselves. Aeschines had used Batalus (1.131), a name that implies effeminacy, to refer to Demosthenes. But here Demosthenes uses it to refer to himself when describing the courageous role that he played in politics, where his actions show that he would be justly called, not Batalus, but whatever name denotes the opposite concept. He refers to Aeschines as Oenomaus, a name that has heroic and tragic connotations, in a situation in which he acted basely and cowardly. Thereby he shows that he obviously deserved another name that has very different connotations. Whether this also involves an element of jest is another question. But in any case this approach of Indignation is a special characteristic of irony.

One must also realize that every ironic statement is not equally in- 366 dignant, but I think that that is obvious from what I have already said. Whenever a speaker uses irony about himself, and especially if he is addressing himself to the jurors rather than to his opponent, he creates pure Indignation, as in the example quoted from Demosthenes earlier: "Perhaps someone wants to think me mad. For it is probably madness to attempt something beyond one's means." There is remarkable Indignation in this passage. But whenever a speaker uses irony against his opponents, the passage primarily reveals Character. This also produces a small element of Indignation, but it is very slight, as in the passage already quoted: "What is your position because of these worthy men?"

In rhetorical exercises known as figured problems (*eschēmatismenon zētēma*),[27] which naturally lend themselves to an indignant style, the Indignation can be quite remarkable, as far as the approach is concerned, whether the speaker uses irony against himself or uses it against his opponent. For example, take the figured problem involving Themistocles when the Athenians decide to sell the ships to rebuild the city. Themistocles speaks against the proposal but is defeated and gives himself up to justice (*prosangellein*).[28] The student will have him say that everything that he had done for which he was admired warranted a condemnation of death. Indeed that he alone understood the oracle made him worthy, not of honor, but of dishonor, because there was no need for the ships; and that he was seen to be victorious in the sea battles likewise did not give him honor, and other things similarly. He will add that those citizens who had persuaded the people to sell the ships are the ones who are admired and that they alone know what is beneficial to the city. Moreover, he will argue that Fortune made a mistake when she 367 did not allow those who had opposed him to be triumphant from the outset, when he persuaded the citizens to take those actions for which he now passes a sentence of death upon himself. He will say that they should not have abandoned the city or done any of the other things that he had recommended. And he will add Indignation by saying too that Cyrsilus should not have been stoned to death but should have been crowned,[29] and that they will live more safely now that they have sold their ships. Because they have been deprived of their ships, he will argue, neither the king of Persia nor anyone else will plot against them. For, he will point out, Greece was saved by the infantry and the fleet was seen to be insignificant in the hour of need. In general, throughout his argument he will demonstrate an idea by saying just the opposite, which is typical of irony and which produces Indignation.

It is characteristic of Indignation to seem perplexed (*ek diaporēseōs*) and thus to call into question matters that are agreed upon as if they were in dispute. This is not very different from irony: "Do I seem to have brought only slight help to those of you who are poor?" etc. (18.107) and, as Thucydides says, "Do we seem to you to be worthy, Spartans?" (1.75). To show any hesitation about what is agreed upon produces the same effect, and we pointed out that this is also characteristic of an un-affected style: "If in respect to those matters in which you were honored one of you committed an injustice, by how much more would you be hated justly, rather than delivered?" (19.238). And then there is the expression of hesitation (*endoiasis*) coupled with the expression of a strong opinion (*epikrisis*): "I think by much." ["I think" shows some hesitation; "by much," a strong opinion.] To show some hesitation about what is agreed upon involves the use of irony.

To judge something as being necessary when you really want to demonstrate that it is not necessary has the same effect: "Since I am going, as it seems, to give an account today of my whole private life and political career" (18.8). He uses the expression "as it seems," which expresses an opinion that involves some hesitation (*epikrisis endoiastikē*), to indicate that he has come into court unwillingly and only because he has been compelled to do so by Aeschines. And do not be surprised if the thought is also introduced in a forceful way, which is surely his intention when he shows that he speaks only out of necessity and because he has been forced to do so by his opponent. As I have said often, almost every passage in Demosthenes is forceful. For the moment we must consider whether this passage also reveals Indignation. That is the type that we are now discussing. Next, as we have often promised, we shall deal with Force. Indeed the natural place to treat Force is after all the other types that have already been discussed, even though its importance would warrant a position ahead of them all. In any case, these are the thoughts and the approaches that are characteristic of Indignation.

There is no diction or other stylistic matter that is typical of Indig-

368

nation. I would say that whatever elements are appropriate in those types that reveal Character, in other words, Simplicity and Modesty and also an unaffected and spontaneous style, are more appropriate here than those features that produce the other styles.

Force (*Deinotēs*)

9 In my opinion Force in a speech is nothing other than the proper use of all the kinds of style previously discussed and of their opposites and of whatever other elements are used to create the body of a speech. To 369 know what technique must be used and when and how it should be used, and to be able to employ all the kinds of style and their opposites and to know what kinds of proofs and thoughts are suitable in the proemium or in the narration or in the conclusion, in other words, as I said, to be able to use all those elements that create the body of a speech as and when they should be used seems to me to be the essence of true Force. Just as a man who properly uses the relevant circumstances that comprise, as it were, the substance of his craft is said to be forceful or clever at that craft, and a general who knows how to manipulate properly the circumstances that fall within the general's expertise (for that is the substance of his craft) receives the same praise, so too an orator who properly uses the circumstances of rhetoric and its material would be considered forceful. What he must know how to manipulate are all those elements that we have already discussed, that is, the kinds of style, etc.. For if any speaker knows when he should use each particular style and when he should not and where he should use it and for how long and against whom and how and why, and if he not only knows but also can apply his knowledge, he will be the most forceful of orators and will 370 surpass all others, just as Demosthenes did. If someone says that a poet is forceful or clever, as Theocritus says of Simonides in the poem *The Graces of Hieron* (16.44), "Unless the clever Cean poet uttering fast-moving words to the accompaniment of his many-stringed lyre had made them famous among men," what he is saying is simply that this poet knew how to use the kinds of style that are appropriate in poetry and had the technical expertise to produce them. Theocritus does not call Simonides a clever or forceful poet in the same sense that people commonly call an orator forceful who uses deep or complicated thoughts or approaches or words that are grand or some similar feature of oratory. But suppose someone wants to argue with us about the word "forceful" (*deinos*) and say that a forceful orator is one who is feared or great or powerful or all these things. Of course we know that the ancients used the word *deinos* in the sense of "feared," as we see in the following passages from Homer's *Iliad*: "You are august and terrible (*deinos*) in my sight, dear father-in-law" (3.172) and "fearful (*deinē*) and terrible to look on" (5.742). They also used it in the sense of "great" and "power-ful": "And in her face she terribly resembles the immortal goddesses" (*Il.* 3.158). But to confirm my own point of view I could add what Homer says about Odysseus. When he wants to show that he was a forceful orator he portrays him as being awesome and great in his use of language, saying that he uttered words that "were similar to winter snowflakes" (3.222). If someone points this passage out to me and argues about our use of the word *deinos*, first of all, he is obviously unaware that Homer here shows Odysseus as being a forceful speaker 371 in the same sense in which I use the word. For to Homer Odysseus used Grandeur and Asperity and Vehemence when and as they should be used, since the speech against Paris and the Trojans required a re-proachful tone. And what will my opponent say about the phrases used to describe Odysseus' speech in Book 8 of the *Odyssey*: "with sweet modesty" (172) and "the god puts a crown of beauty on his words" (170)? If he argues that this is not typical of Force, but is something else, what will he say about what Odysseus says when he is among the Phaeacians? The same man is speaking in this passage and in the one cited earlier, but he does not use speech in the same way since he is really a forceful speaker and can thus use the types of style when and as they should be used. If he is making a charge about the use of violence, rape, adultery, transgression of law, impiety against Zeus who protects the guest-host relationship, and other accusations that anyone could make against Paris and the Trojans, one would expect him to produce "a great voice from his chest" and "words similar to winter snowflakes" (*Il.* 3.221–222) and, in general, to be grand and vehement and lofty in his speech. But if, because of their generosity toward him, he wants to praise and put in a good humor men who love pleasure, he does not speak in this way but says: "I, indeed, say that nothing is more delightful / than when joy fills a whole people," etc. (*Od.* 9.5–6). Thus by addressing people in a suitable way the orator will prod "one with gentle words, another with harsh words" (*Il.* 12.267).

So, what will the man who disagrees with us about the use of the word "force" say about these passages? Was the same man forceful at times, but not at others? I would argue that the same man is speaking in all these passages and is using the same Force and the same craft, since he knows that it is necessary to use different kinds of style and is able to do so. And why should I give other examples since it is possible to see this in Demosthenes? That same man is forceful in every passage that he wrote, using the same unified skill and the same talent in them all and employing each type of style appropriately. Since he adapts his style to the subject and the occasions and the personages involved, he projects one image in the private speeches and another in his public speeches. Even in the public speeches he does not appear to be the same in the speeches against Philip as he does in the other deliberative speeches. But what he says is always appropriate. If at one time he appears to be forceful and at another he does not, this itself is exactly what is forceful about his speeches. It is typical of real Force to be knowledgeable enough to project any impression that the situation demands. This is what we must now discuss.

One kind of forceful speech is one that is both forceful and appears to be so. Most people, and perhaps those who would argue with us about the use of the term "force," say that only a speech that appears to be forceful has Force. This will soon be clarified in the discussion that follows. As we were saying, one type of forceful speech is one that is both forceful and appears to be so. There are also speeches that are forceful but do not seem to be so, and those that seem to be forceful but in fact are not.[30] Obviously it would be a waste of time to deal with a speech that neither is in fact, nor seems to be, forceful. A speech that seems to be forceful and is so in fact is produced by the thought and all the other elements that create the various kinds of style. One that is forceful but does not seem to be so is usually produced by the approach. And one that seems to be forceful but is not so in fact is usually created by the diction.

The *Philippics* and almost all the speeches delivered against Philip as

372

373

well as the majority of the public orations are examples of a style that
both is and seems to be forceful. In these speeches Demosthenes wants
to seem to be a forceful speaker, and indeed he admits (6.44–45) that he
is emulating Pericles, who was obviously very forceful as a speaker.
And in these speeches he not only seems forceful but is so in fact. He is
forceful in these orations, as in all his other speeches, because he used a
certain kind of style when and as it should be used. Here he has made
an open display of this Force, since these speeches required it. We cannot discuss now why that is so, since we must return to the point that
we were making. In these speeches he is in fact forceful and appears
and seems to be forceful because he says what he has to say in such a
way that all realize that his sentiments have not been expressed in an
ordinary way, either in reference to the thoughts, or to the other elements of style that we have discussed.

Thus thoughts that are typical of this sort of Force are paradoxical,
profound, compelling, or, in general, any cleverly contrived thoughts:
"Yet it is reasonable to suppose, men of Athens, that that aspect of
Philip's situation that is most difficult to combat is also best for you"
(1.4) or "What is worst from times gone by is best as far as the future is
concerned" (4.2). There is also an especially compelling passage in the
speech *On the False Embassy*: "I deny that I served on the embassy
with you; but I do say that you did many things on the embassy that
were terrible, and I served the best interests of these citizens" (189).
There is another passage in the speech *On the Crown* that is cleverly
expressed: "It will be clear from those parts of the decree that he does
not indict that he is vindictive in indicting other parts of it" (118) or
"These, then, are my donations, which you did not indict. But you
prosecute as illegal those honors that the Council says I ought to receive
in return for them" (119). The enthymeme that follows is also forceful:
"Therefore, do you admit that it is lawful to receive gifts, but prosecute
showing gratitude for them on the grounds that that is illegal?" (119).
This whole section of the speech has been cleverly contrived. In effect
he is saying, "Since you did not reproach the gift, you admit that it is
also lawful to receive gratitude for it. For if the gift is not illegal, gratitude for it is surely not." At least that is his basic idea. But neither the
approach nor the expression of his thought appears to be forceful at all,
although each one is in fact; they seem rather to be sincere and to reveal

374

Character and to be composed in a beautiful and vehement manner.[31] It is clear from what follows in the speech that these passages are vehement and reveal Character and have been introduced in this way at the right moment. Thus these and similar thoughts are characteristic of a speech that is truly forceful and seems to be so. In addition to these almost all those thoughts that produce Grandeur, that is, those that create Florescence, Solemnity, and the rest, are appropriate.

375

Appropriate approaches are those that resemble the thoughts already discussed, that is, those that are ingenious and profound. All those that are typical of those types that create Grandeur are also appropriate. That is why most people think that only these styles are forceful. Likewise the diction that is characteristic of these types is suitable in the kind of style that is and seems to be forceful. Solemn words and words that are harsh and vehement and, generally speaking, words that are used figuratively are forceful, because it is appropriate to use them whenever you want to describe something vividly, and because of that they seem to be typical of Force.

But the figures and the word order and all the other elements that are characteristic of Force are not those that are typical of those types that produce Grandeur, but those that are appropriate to Solemnity and Florescence and Brilliance and Abundance. The figure that involves concentrating many thoughts concisely into one sentence (*to kata systrophēn schēma*) is especially suitable. Demosthenes' use of this figure clearly shows great natural ability: "How could the man who ordered the Spartans to give up Messene and then handed over Orchomenus and Coroneia to the Thebans be considered to have done these things because he thought that they were just?" (6.13) or "He who does and prepares those things by which I might be captured," etc. (9.17) or "If, when we came to bring help to the Euboeans" (1.8). There are other similar examples. This is what a style that both is and seems to be forceful is like.

376

Almost all the private speeches of Demosthenes are examples of a style that does not seem to be forceful but that is so in fact. Quite a few parts of the public speeches are also like this. And one could say with confidence that all the speeches of Lysias are of this sort. This kind of Force is not produced by the thought but, as I said before, is created primarily—in fact totally—by the approach. This will be clear from the examples. I think that it is characteristic of a very forceful speech, but one that does not seem to be forceful, for someone to seem to speak naturally and simply and in an artless manner, and thus to downplay the significance of what he says by using commonplace thoughts and conversational diction—and in diction I include all those features of style such as figures, clauses, word order, cadences, and rhythms that are related to it. To prove whatever point you want to make in this way rather than by seeming to speak in an artificial and complex manner, and to use this style in the proemium and in the narration and in the other parts of the speech, is typical of the kind of Force that I am now discussing. It is also characteristic of the really forceful style that certain passages seem simple and the style itself seems to be natural, although

377 both it and its aims are in fact quite the opposite.[32] But such a speech could not be elevated or grand nor could it be forceful in every respect if it were constructed throughout in this way, since a speech often needs some element of strength and depth and Grandeur, which Demosthenes injects even into the private speeches. Lysias and his followers use these elements less often, if one is to judge conservatively; for if we must discuss these orators, it is pretty clear that they use these styles seldom or not at all. In any case these are two kinds of Force.

The style of the sophists, that is, of Polus and Gorgias and Meno and their followers, and of quite a few in our own times (I need not name them all), is the sort that appears to be forceful but is not really so, which is, as I said, the third kind of Force. This is created primarily by the diction, when a speaker uses rough and vehement or even solemn words to express thoughts that are shallow and commonplace. This is especially true if he also uses figures of speech and clauses and some or all of the other aspects of style that are typical of Beauty and Florescence and Solemnity. Moreover, it is typical of a style that appears to be forceful, but is not, to utter reproaches and vehement attacks at random before showing that they are justified, or to use them where they are unnecessary, as Aristogiton usually does. This is typical of sloppy composition and is artificial. Also, if a speaker uses thoughts or even approaches that produce Grandeur, such as those that are typical

378 of Solemnity or Vehemence or Asperity or Brilliance or Florescence or even Abundance, but does not employ these at the right time or in the right place, the speech will appear to be forceful but will not really be

so. I agree that it can be useful at times to employ a grand style in dealing with some slight and insignificant matter, and even Isocrates (*Paneg.* 8) says that it is one of the duties of an orator to be able to treat insignificant matters in a grand way and significant matters slightingly. But that is useful only when it is done at the right time, and this sense of propriety is even more crucial here than it is with other types of style. And this, I think, is the essence of great and consummate knowledge, to know when to use an appropriate style and to be able to do it. That is really what Force is, as I said at the beginning of my discussion: to know how to use all the kinds of style and all kinds of thoughts and to understand when and where and against whom and how and in what circumstances they should be used. The orator must not only understand this, but also be able to put into practice what he understands. This is a topic that is worthy of a special treatment following our discussion *On Types of Style*, arranged separately on its own, just as our discussion *On Types of Style* followed the one *On Invention.*[33]

I have not been totally led astray from the discussion of Force. But I did not choose to make such a discussion a secondary topic of another treatment and did not deal with it by way of an appendix, as would have been the case if I had treated it now, but gave it the separate treatment that it deserves. The reader must not be discontent because of that. As we were writing this discussion *On Types of Style*, from time to time we promised to deal with some topic "in the discussion of Force," 379 but we were thinking of this separate treatise just mentioned. Anyone who has tried to deal with this topic will know what an overwhelming task it is. To treat all the problems involved in this subject in a systematic way seems almost beyond human ability and to require some divine power. One would have to deal with times, characters, places, causes, manners, and other such topics[34] and to discuss all the possible cases, as well as the various forms that they can take and the ways in which they can be presented, and what kinds of sentiments are appropriate in each part of the speech, in the proemium or in the confirmation or in the refutation or in the epilogue. It would be necessary to treat all the types of style and to discuss what kind of style is generally appropriate to each particular problem, depending on the men involved and the character about whom they are talking and the moment at which they are speaking. One would also have to discuss what sentiments can be used in each part of the speech and, of those that have been discovered, which ones should be included and which ones would be better left out, and that would depend on the circumstances of the case. It would also be necessary to deal with the best order in which to present the points that the orator has decided to make in one case or another; this too will depend on the circumstances of the case. One would also have to deal with how one point or another should be introduced and what thoughts should be expanded and what is the best way to do this, as well as which ones should be passed over as quickly as possible. I think that it requires divine rather than human ability to deal with all these matters and those questions that are related to them in a systematic discussion 380 that is not too long. To the limit of our human ability, I think that we shall be up to this task and shall deal with all these topics in a satisfactory way in the treatise *On the Approach of Force*, to which we shall turn our attention as soon as we have finished this discussion.

But first we must deal with practical oratory and the individuals who have been famous orators, not all of them, of course, but only the best. If the reader has understood our previous general discussion of the various types of style, it will not be difficult for him to understand what must be appreciated about each of the orators discussed, whether they lived in recent times or long ago. So now we must discuss practical oratory.

Practical Oratory (*Logos Politikos*)

10 A so-called practical speech is one that is composed out of all the types of style previously discussed, not used one by one, but in some way blended with one another, as we said earlier. The orator who effects the best blend of these styles will create the best practical speech, and the one who effects the second-best blend will produce the second-best practical speech, and the third-best blend will produce the third-best, and so forth. No one will dispute our contention that Demosthenes produces the best mixture of these styles and that his oratory is the best practical oratory. But our task now is not to discuss Demosthenes, but to deal with the best practical oratory, so that from this discussion it 381 will be easy for us to characterize those individuals who were famous as practicing orators. However, if you discuss the best practical oratory, you will seem by necessity to be discussing Demosthenes, for the two are interchangeable. The best practical oratory is that of Demosthenes, and the oratory of Demosthenes, in turn, is the best practical oratory.

I would argue that in such a speech the kind of style that creates Clarity and that reveals Character and that conveys Sincerity must be predominant. Next in importance would be Rapidity; then, of those types that create Grandeur, Abundance must be used frequently throughout the speech, as well as Purity and Distinctness. Moreover, Asperity and Vehemence must in some way be given a place comparable to the styles already mentioned, although these are second and third in importance. Florescence and then Solemnity and also Brilliance ought to be used, but not as much as the types mentioned earlier. In fact Florescence and Brilliance should be used less than these, seeing that one should break up Solemnity in practical speeches and make it less grand, as in the following example: "All the life of men, whether they live in a large or a small city, is governed by nature and by laws" (25.15). By putting in the parenthesis, "whether they live in a large or a small city," and thus interrupting the flow of the sentence, Demosthenes has made the passage appear to be less grand and less solemn. This same thing can happen in a brilliant passage, as another example from Demosthenes shows: "This was the beginning and the first basis of negotiations with Thebes" (18.188); then, before introducing a phrase that would have made the passage very brilliant and sophistic, that is, "This decree made the danger surrounding the city disappear like a cloud," he cut up the 382 thought and made it appear less brilliant by introducing the parenthesis, "and these negotiations previously had been characterized by animosity and hatred and lack of trust because of these men."

Thus in the best political oration Grandeur ought to be present, but only up to a point and in the way that I have described. There is little need for the kind of Force that both is and appears to be forceful, very much for that which is forceful but does not seem to be so, that is, the kind that revolves primarily around the approach, and none at all for the kind that only appears to be forceful, unless someone might consider brilliant and florescent passages to be of this sort. I said that I would treat the approach of Force in a separate treatise. (We have already discussed the importance of different kinds of Force in practical oratory.)

A practical oration should always possess Beauty, which, as we said, is used for embellishment. It should not be overly obvious, but should be used as it is in the speeches of Demosthenes. We discussed that in our treatment of Beauty. However, where there is a need for close arguments and careful reasoning, it is appropriate to employ frequently the rhythms, word order, and cadences that are typical of Beauty. The pains taken with the style are useful in expressing ideas that demand close attention, since the Purity of the word order and the cadence makes such ideas and discussions not seem overly dry, but adds a charm of its own and rouses the audience up and does not allow them to be vexed or troubled by the use of ideas that are densely packed together. Passages

383 that involve argumentation also require the blandishments that can be conferred on a passage by style. It is the function of style to be able to express clearly and in a very few words many ideas or ideas that are difficult to comprehend or many obscure ideas without lapsing into some stylistic defect such as excessive simplicity (*euteleia*) or stiffness (*sclērotēs*), and to do this brevity needs an element of Beauty, which is what the well-wrought style produces. Moreover, a well-wrought and carefully composed style is a defense against excessive simplicity. And so, even if because of the carefully reasoned nature of the thoughts the style becomes excessively simple, as often happens in such passages, you can perk it up by using figures and rhythms and the word order and cadences that are associated with Beauty.

We shall discuss fully in the treatise *On the Approach of Force* when and how certain types of style should predominate in a speech. Now we are simply discussing political oratory and the style of Demosthenes in general rather than any particular Demosthenic oration or any particular practical speech. There is a difference between discussing something in a general way and discussing it in parts. The public speeches of Demosthenes and the private speeches and, of the public speeches, the speech *Against Leptines* and the speech *On the Crown* are all, to be sure, by Demosthenes, but they are very different from one another because there are different predominant styles in them. In some situations there is good reason to employ to a greater extent certain kinds of style such as Asperity or Modesty or a style that reveals Character or one of the others. But the purely Demosthenic style, that is to say, the most beautiful kind of practical oratory, is created in another way, namely, by

384 that blending and mixture of styles that we outlined earlier. That is, in

Demosthenic oratory the sort of style that produces Clarity and reveals Character and conveys Sincerity predominates. Rapidity and Abundance are used in similar proportions; and Asperity and Vehemence are also employed, but less than Abundance. They are, in fact, on a second and third level of importance compared with the styles mentioned earlier. Solemnity and Brilliance and Florescence are also used, but even less than the styles already discussed. The kind of Force that revolves around the approach is used very often, but the other is employed very little or hardly at all. Beauty, which adds embellishment to a speech, is used almost as often as the styles that I mentioned first, especially when it is necessary to make a statement effectively, unemphatically, and without obvious contrivance. Thus it is by blending all these elements that the most beautiful practical oratory, which is that of Demosthenes, is produced.

There are three kinds of practical oratory: the deliberative, the judicial, and the panegyric. In deliberative oratory, obviously the kinds of style that create Grandeur predominate, along with that sort of Force that both is and seems to be forceful. Deliberative oratory must appear to have Force, in addition to being forceful, because it ought to be dignified as well as possess the other qualities that, in our opinion, the most beautiful practical oratory ought to have. It will also employ in moderate proportions the style that reveals Character, with the exception of Indignation and the kind of Vehemence that involves the use of irony. The reader should not be surprised at what I have said, even if some deliberative speeches, such as those of Demosthenes, that naturally belong to this category reveal quite a lot of Character and Modesty. At the moment we are not describing his speeches individually, as we have often pointed out, but the kind of style that generally distinguishes a 385 deliberative speech, such as that which one sees in the *Philippics*. So even if some special features of the persons involved in the situation, or some other factor, causes a deliberative oration such as the speech *For the Megalopolitans* or some other to be less dignified than a deliberative speech normally would be and to reveal Character more fully, that does not vitiate our argument about what qualities the best deliberative speech should possess. In other words, it should, as we have pointed out, be dignified and show a preference for those styles that we mentioned. A deliberative oration that for some reason is prevented from exhibiting those qualities that are characteristic of the best deliberative oratory would not be an appropriate example of the best deliberative speech. And if someone should say that even the *Philippics* assume a grand tone because of the Character of Philip and that he is the object of the criticism and the Vehemence in these speeches, he should consider how much Asperity and Florescence is directed against the Athenians in these orations and how much frankness and Grandeur they exhibit, even apart from the Character of Philip. Of course we would have to agree that the Character of Philip also contributes to the tone of these speeches, but it does not contribute as much as does the particular form that Demosthenes' advice takes. But our treatise *On the Approach of Force* will discuss more fully the effect that characters and occasions have on a speech. The most beautiful deliberative speech is such as we have described.

The most admirable judicial speech is just the opposite, unless it is one that deals with public affairs and important issues and resembles the advice that one finds in deliberative speeches. The speeches *Against Aristocrates* and *On the Crown* and others are good examples of this kind of judicial speech. These exhibit characteristics that are like those that one finds in a deliberative speech, and perhaps they should not even be considered to be speeches that are judicial in nature. In any case, although it is not true of these speeches, a true judicial speech is, as I said, the opposite of a deliberative speech. It should above all use a style that reveals Character and Modesty and one that is simple. It should possess very little Indignation or any other similar style or, at least, it should use it as seldom as possible. But it admits the sort of Grandeur that is produced by Abundance in reference to the thoughts. Abundance that is produced by diction or other stylistic features or by the approach used is not appropriate except on rare occasions. Nor is the sort of Grandeur produced by the other types acceptable except, on occasion, the sort of Vehemence that is produced by the thought or the diction, which includes those figures that are related to diction. It employs the other aspects of a practical speech just as a deliberative speech does. Such are the judicial speeches of Demosthenes, by which I mean the private speeches.

The most beautiful of panegyric styles in prose is surely that of Plato. I do not mean panegyric passages in practical cases, but pure panegyric,

386

which perhaps would not even be called practical oratory. And just as we said that the most beautiful kind of practical oratory is synonymous with that of Demosthenes, so we could say here that the most beautiful kind of panegyric oratory is synonymous with the style of Plato. Just as in the case of practical oratory the style of Demosthenes is interchangeable with the best practical style, the same is true with panegyric oratory and Plato. For the most beautiful of panegyric styles is that of Plato, and the style of Plato is the most beautiful of panegyric styles in prose. That is what we must now discuss. We shall deal a little later with 387 panegyric elements in practical oratory, which anyone would agree would naturally be discussed after our treatment of deliberative and judicial oratory. But we cannot do that now.

The most beautiful panegyric style, which in our opinion is that of Plato, is produced by using all the types that create Grandeur, except Asperity and Vehemence. But they must be accompanied by Simplicity, which quantitatively should not be less than they are. It should not be used, however, when it is clear that the passage should be elevated and solemn. The stylistic delights produced by Sweetness are especially appropriate in a panegyric speech, even though they can sometimes be used in other kinds of oratory, as well as those elements of a carefully wrought style that make the passage pretty and charming. In panegyric oratory the kind of Force that involves the approach, that is, the one that is least apparent, occurs everywhere. The other kind is never appropriate in panegyric oratory unless some character of those who go to make up the author's panegyric work wants to demonstrate exactly this kind of Force, as Socrates is depicted by Plato to have done when he wanted to demonstrate to Phaedrus the Force that resides primarily in style (*Phdr.* 237). He thus compares and contrasts his own speech with that of Lysias. Plato obviously does the same thing in other works with reference to other characters in accordance with the imitative element in the panegyric manner.

Since panegyric is almost entirely narrative, the style should avoid Rapidity. But it employs the other kinds of style or ingredients of a 388 practical oration more or less in the way deliberative speeches and judicial speeches use them. In panegyric speeches that involve replies from other speakers or an element of dialogue, such as those that one often finds in Plato, harsh passages and vehement passages are not at all out of place, nor in fact is any sort of Force. Some of the speeches of Polus in the *Gorgias* possess the kind of Force that appears to be forceful but is not really. And passages that involve a dialogue of some sort not only admit these kinds of style already mentioned but also every kind of style, because these passages imitate reality and are dramatic and are constructed in such a way that the various kinds of style are separated from one another and are not mixed together. You might find, for example, a distinct passage that is simple, and a separate passage that is solemn, and each of the other styles used in different passages. You could even find the kind of style that is conversational and reflects the language of everyday life. For a realistic representation of people allows even this style.

A panegyric speech in prose ought to be similar to what we have described. But in practical cases in which there is a need for the kind of panegyric that is appropriate to a real case, which I promised a little earlier to discuss, panegyric passages are not like those that I have been describing, but are of a more practical nature and should be constructed out of almost the same elements that make up a deliberative speech, except that Brilliance and Solemnity ought to be used in these passages more often than in a real deliberative speech. For there are certain situations that demand both practical oratory and panegyric, such as if the Athenians and the Spartans should argue after the Persian Wars about who should have the first place in a procession, or some similar 389 situation. But we must return to our discussion. This is how a practical speech that has panegyric overtones should be constructed. The style of Plato is the most beautiful of panegyric styles in prose, and we would recommend this, as the best example to follow, to anyone who is willing and able to construct a panegyric speech.

All poetry is panegyric and is, in fact, the most panegyric of all literary styles. Therefore, we must discuss what is the most effective kind of poetry, as we discussed what is the most effective kind of panegyric. But first we must describe this, just as we described all the other general kinds of style, by discussing the most beautiful manifestations of them. Our organization here will not be like that which we have previously followed, since we must add many other observations to everything that has already been said about panegyric oratory, and anyone would readily agree that these observations that we must now make really apply primarily to poetry. Here we must also repeat what we said earlier and keep the same "proportion," to use the geometric term: what, in our opinion, Demosthenes is to practical oratory, both deliberative and judicial, and Plato is to panegyric oratory in prose, Homer is to poetry. If anyone says that poetry is panegyric in meter, I cannot say that he is mistaken. Here you could simply invert the propositions as we did in the case of Plato and Demosthenes: the best poetry is that of Homer, and Homer is the best of poets. I would say that he is also the best of orators and speech-writers, although perhaps this is implicit in what I have already said. Poetry is an imitation of all things. The man who best imitates, in a suitable style, both orators delivering speeches and singers singing panegyrics, such as Phemius and Demodocus and other characters engaged in every pursuit, this man is the best poet. Since this is the case, perhaps by saying that Homer is the best of poets I have made a statement that is tantamount to saying that he is also the best of orators and the best of speech-writers. He is perhaps not the best general or craftsman or other such professional,[35] although he represents their pursuits in the best way. Their skill does not reside in the use of speech and words. But as for those whose business is with the use of speech, such as orators and speech-writers, the one who represents them best and describes how the best of them would speak, is surely himself the best of them. Thus of all poets and orators and speech-writers Homer is the best at using every kind of style. Indeed he is the man who more than any other poet has created passages of Grandeur and those that produce pleasure and those that exhibit a carefully wrought style and Force. He has also produced a vivid representation of reality that is suitable to the circumstances that he is describing, both in the style that he uses and in the way he presents his characters, as well as in vivid narrations of mythical stories. He uses different kinds of caesura, or pauses in the line of verse, in his poetry, and as a result of this the verses are varied. And a sense of propriety in reference to a specific passage always governs the various kinds of verse that he uses. Moreover, he has also chosen a meter that is by nature the most noble of them all. Finally, he has turned variety and diversity into the most beautiful unity. These comments are sufficient to characterize the best kind of poetry and Homer himself. Let us return to our original point in order to fill out the discussion that we began there.

390

391

So far as poetry is concerned, the most admirable of panegyric speeches is created out of all those elements that we mentioned before in our discussion of panegyric oratory, used as we described them, and, in addition to these, those features that are typical of poetry. Judicial and deliberative oratory employ these characteristics of poetry to a very limited extent, or very seldom, and use only some of them rather than all of them. But a panegyric speech in prose employs almost all of them, although they are always toned down somewhat and are never used as openly as they would be in poetry. In comparison with other literature, the use of meter, both meters as technically understood and those that can be perceived by the naked ear, is typical of poetry. And all mythical thoughts are typical of poetry, such as the stories about Cronos and the Titans and the Giants and Zeus himself and the other gods, narrated as if they had human feelings and describing how they were born and what they have done or do, either among themselves or in their dealings with human beings, and their love-affairs and wars and friendships and their births and how they live and other such aspects of their existence. In addition poets narrate marvels about men or other animals—how Cadmus was changed from a man into a snake and how Halcyon became a bird, and stories about nightingales and swallows. It is also typical of poetry to describe how men such as Teiresias became women and women such as Caenis became men, and to depict winged men and how they were produced and all sorts of animals that are put together in a strange way, such as the Pegasuses and the Gorgons and the Centaurs and the Sirens and the Titans and the Lastrygones and the Cyclopes and Perseus and other such creatures. Stories that exaggerate the natural abilities of men and tell of marvels done by them as though they were worthy of belief are also mythical and typical of poetry. Stories about how far Achilles jumped or how easy it was for Ajax or Hector to throw a stone a great distance or how great these men were, and other stories of this kind, are characteristic of poetry. It is also typical of poetry to depict inanimate objects as serving the gods as if they were beings that have feelings and perception, as in the following examples from Homer's *Iliad*: "The gates of heaven groaned open of their own accord" (5.749) and "For them the divine earth produced" (14.347). In general poetry indulges in marvelous stories that are impossible and unbelievable. But the line from the *Iliad*, "The sea monsters skipped in childish glee under

392

him" (13.27), and other such passages are poetical and produce pleasure, as we said in our discussion of Sweetness, but they have less of a marvelous quality, unless one would argue that it is exceedingly mythical and poetical for horses or other animals to utter human sounds. It is also typical of Simplicity and of poetry to describe gracefully some particular detail of a general situation, such as in the following passage from the *Iliad*: "The smell of the burnt sacrifice went up to heaven, whirling in the smoke" (1.317). Homer does the same thing in Book 5 of the *Iliad* when he says that one man killed another in such a way that "tumbling, he fell into the dust" (586) and that "he was breathing hard" (585) and other such passages. Passages like this are useful in poetry, but seem out of place in history, unless someone should wish to write history in a very simple way—for details can be both simple and sweet. These, then, are the thoughts that are characteristic of poetry in addition to the other thoughts that are appropriate in a panegyric speech, which are also appropriate in poetry.[36]

    393

In addition to the approaches that are typical of panegyric oratory there is one that is especially characteristic of poetry, and that is when poets do not seem to tell their story on their own authority but call upon the Muses or Apollo or some other god to help them, and thus make it seem that their account comes from a divine source. Judicial and deliberative speeches almost never use this approach. Panegyric speeches do, but always with a measure of apology.[37]

It should be clear to everyone what kind of diction is typical of poetry, and that the most beautiful of poetic dictions is that of Homer. His diction is probably the only one that is pure, so far as poetry allows, with the possible exception of Hesiod. Unlike the thoughts and at least one approach and the diction, there are no figures that are particularly characteristic of poetry, but it uses the same ones that are typical of panegyric oratory, although their use is determined by the demands of various styles required by the nature of what is being represented [since poetry is a representation of reality].

It is easy to see that the clauses and word order and rhythms and cadences that are typical of poetry are determined by the meter, and one can see that this is true so long as the poetry is nothing but verse. But when we discuss Homer, we must add that we cannot describe his meter simply by saying that it is a dactylic hexameter catalectic. Nor

    394

can we say that Homer uses one kind of cadence or rhythm or word order. Just as we said that various figures must be used because epic poetry is a representation of reality, so the same observation could be made in the case of the meter used. Whenever Homer describes the emotional state of a speaker or imitates some peculiar characteristic of a person in the poem or even narrates various deeds on his own, in each of these situations he must vary the kind of style that he uses and employ appropriate cadences and feet and word order and rhythms, so that he can produce passages that are solemn or harsh or simple or very beautiful and carefully wrought or that illustrate any other kinds of rhythm and styles that we have discussed. These various effects are easily produced because of the large number of patterns that a hexameter can take—the grammarians teach us that there are thirty-two.[38] The effect produced also depends on what kind of cadence is used, and that is very important in such questions. Often a metrical impression that is different from what one expects in epic poetry is produced because of the logical divisions within the line of poetry and the cadences of the clauses in which a thought is completed. Take the following line, for example, from the *Iliad*: *hērōōn, autous de helōria teuche kynessin* ("of warriors, and made themselves spoils for the dogs," 1.4). That the preceding clause is completed at the beginning of this line, with the word *hērōōn*, produces the same impression that an anapaest does. Anyone who has carefully studied all my previous comments about the various types of style would have no difficulty in understanding why this rhythm is necessary in this passage or why some other rhythm is appropriate in another passage. This will be even clearer to anyone who has also studied our discussion about the approach that is characteristic of Force, which follows this treatise.

395

Now we must discuss those writers who rank below each of the three that we have already discussed and who win, as it were, the second and third prizes in the kinds of oratory that they practiced. We shall discuss practical oratory first. But before that we must discuss briefly what pure practical oratory is, as opposed to that which was practiced by Demosthenes or some other orator, and what pure panegyric oratory is, as opposed to the most beautiful kind, which is that of Plato and Homer. And we must describe briefly the men who excelled in one kind of oratory or another. Judicial oratory has been dealt with sufficiently. We proceed, therefore, as we said, with our discussion of pure practical oratory.

Pure Practical Oratory (*Haplōs Politikos*)

11   The style that could be described as being purely practical is one that is produced by those types that create Clarity in the speech, as well as the types that reveal a modest and simple Character and the type that makes the style unaffected, because this is conducive to persuasion. All these styles should be understood as a unity: the purely practical style is created out of their mixture and combination into one. All the speakers whom we call practical orators use this style, except perhaps Isocrates to a certain extent. Lysias and Isaeus and Hyperides use it extensively, which is why they are so persuasive.

But these orators differ from one another. In Lysias the elements that   396 produce a carefully wrought style are used only moderately, and those that create embellishment or adornment are not very noticeable. There is very little Rapidity, and only a moderate amount of the kind of Abundance that is produced by the thought, and practically none of the sort of Abundance that involves the approach or the diction or stylistic features that are related to the diction. Lysias very rarely uses those styles that make a passage dignified, although there is in his speeches very much of that kind of Force that is created through the approach.

In addition to those elements that create a purely practical speech, the style of Isaeus is characterized by a great deal of Rapidity,[39] which makes it similar to the most beautiful style that one finds in practical oratory. The features that create a carefully wrought style are more striking in his speeches than they are in Lysias, and this is true also of Abundance and the other kinds of style that create Grandeur. There is also a hint of Florescence in his style. In the use of these styles he falls far short of Demosthenes but is far superior to Lysias. In his works there is also a lot of the sort of Force that involves the approach, but Lysias is more forceful in this respect.

The style of Hyperides is hardly carefully wrought, which is why in some ways it does not seem to be very powerful. But there is swollen Grandeur in his speeches, and the grand passages are stiff and not well integrated into the rest of the speech. They are not, in other words, well blended with the style that reveals Character and with Purity. His style is not quick-paced, and there is very little of the sort of Rapidity that is created by figures of speech. His style does exhibit the sort of Force that involves the approach, as does the style of all the other orators. But there is less of this sort of Force in Hyperides than in Lysias and Isaeus and, of course, much less than in Demosthenes, who surpasses both Lysias and Isaeus in this respect. In the speeches of Hyperides you would also find that kind of Force that both is and appears to be forceful, in addition to the kind that depends on the approach. But you would find it rarely, since it is rarely found even in Demosthenes. And it is typical of Hyperides to use words freely and carelessly, as when he says "onliest" and "weasel-trap" and "to cry cuckoo" and "to stele-inscribe" and a "partner in" instead of "acquainted with."[40] There are other examples. However, these orators differ from one another in their use of diction.

397

Now we shall discuss the others, pointing out how each of them uses certain distinctive stylistic features, although they are similar to one another in their use of those characteristics that are seen in all practical oratory. They obviously differ from one another in that they use some particular kind of style more or less often than the others, or employ it only moderately. We shall begin our discussion with Isocrates.

So far as concerns the types that make speech clear, that is, Purity and Distinctness, Isocrates' style is the most practical of all. But because he does not use the style that reveals Character and Sincerity, his speeches are less persuasive than those of other orators. However, his style is exceedingly carefully wrought and beautiful, and he uses abundantly those kinds of style that produce Grandeur, except that he tones down passages that are vehement or harsh, if he ever even uses them, with a carefully wrought style. He does not use very often the sort of Abundance that involves the diction or the approach, although he frequently employs the kind that is related to the thought. There is no Rapidity at all in his speeches. Moreover, although I hate to say it, his style is flatter and more diffuse than that of the other orators. It is in fact the style of an old man and a teacher. Because he does not use those techniques that make the style seem naturally unaffected, his speeches are full of elaborations, as if he wanted to exhibit how he had worked out his thoughts. And he adds a lot of useless comments. This is clear when we compare passages in which Demosthenes deals with the same 398 thoughts but does not elaborate and prove them as fully as Isocrates does. There are many examples of what I mean, but the clearest one is from the proemium of the *First Philippic*: "If it were being proposed to discuss some new topic," etc. If we compare this with the proemium of the *Archidamus* of Isocrates, we see that the same proposition is stated, namely, that young men who rise to speak before their elders should be tolerated. But Isocrates has elaborately and fully worked out the proposition, whereas Demosthenes is content to demonstrate it simply. (We shall have to examine at another time whether the proemium of Isocrates' speech has other defects.) Finally, there is quite a lot of the kind of Force that involves the approach in the style of Isocrates too. This concludes our discussion of Isocrates' style.

Since Dinarchus was a practicing orator, his style is very clear and unaffected and persuasive. It also has a lot of Vehemence and the Asperity that is produced by the thought and the approach. His diction is not very vehement, although in his use of figures, clauses, word order, cadences, and rhythms, all of which are related to the diction, his style is very vehement and harsh. That is why it is also less carefully wrought. But it is quite rapid and forceful, although it seems to be more forceful than it really is because this is the sort of Force that he uses. Generally speaking, Dinarchus employs a style that appears to be very Demosthenic, mainly because it is harsh and rapid and vehement. Some critics, 399 not inappropriately, have said jokingly that he is a "gingerbread Demosthenes."[41] This concludes our discussion of Dinarchus.

The style of Aeschines is typical of practical oratory but has other characteristics. It is pompous and excessive and primarily uses Grandeur and the sort of Beauty that is produced by figures. It is not generally carefully wrought, since a carefully wrought style is not the sort of embellishment that he employs. In fact his style is rarely carefully wrought and is sometimes careless and slack. He depends quite a lot on the style that reveals a modest Character, but employs less often the kind that conveys Sincerity. Because he does not develop his argument with confidence and Sincerity, there are passages in his speeches that have no intensity, although he often uses a vehement and harsh style. This is also the reason his style is not very rapid or quick-paced. In his speeches there is quite a lot of the sort of Force that depends on the approach, and it is clear from what I have said that there is also the kind of Force that both appears to be forceful and really is.

Before discussing Antiphon I must point out that, as Didymus the grammarian and quite a few others say, and as is apparent from history, there were many Antiphons, but two were engaged in rhetorical pur-

400 suits. These are the ones that we must give an account of. One of these is the orator to whom the speeches about homicide, as well as deliberative speeches and other similar works, are attributed. The other one is said to have been a soothsayer and an interpreter of dreams; the speeches *Concerning Truth* and the one *About Concord* and the *Politics* are attributed to him. As far as I am concerned the difference in the types used in these works makes it clear that there were two Antiphons. There is really a great difference between those speeches entitled *Concerning Truth* and the others. Because of this I do not believe Plato and others who say that there was only one Antiphon.[42] I hear from many that Thucydides was a pupil of Antiphon the Rhamnusian, and I know that it is the Rhamnusian to whom the speeches about homicide are attributed. But I do not believe that Thucydides was his pupil, since his style is very different and shows more similarities with the speeches *Concerning Truth.* In any case, whether there was one Antiphon who used two kinds of style that are very different from each other, or two of them, one who used one kind of style and one who used another, we must treat them separately. As we said, there is a tremendous difference between them.

Antiphon the Rhamnusian, to whom are attributed the speeches about homicide, was a practicing orator whose style, consequently, is clear

401 and reveals Sincerity as well as other aspects of Character. Thus his style is also persuasive. But one sees all of these characteristics less in his speeches than in those of the other orators whom we have discussed. He is said to have been the first to pursue this kind of speaking and to have been the founder and originator of the kind of oratory that we call practical. Indeed, as far as chronology is concerned, he is the eldest of all the ten orators.[43] He uses Grandeur quite often, and his grand passages are beautifully woven into the rest of the speech. They are not distinct from other passages, as in Hyperides, or pompous and excessive as in Aeschines, although Antiphon's diction is often elevated. But his

style is so carefully wrought that it is not tedious, and it is moderately rapid and forceful.

The other Antiphon, Antiphon the Sophist, to whom the discourses *Concerning Truth* are attributed, was hardly a practicing orator. His style is solemn and ponderous. This is for several reasons, but especially because in his sentences he tries everything that is characteristic of a dignified style and one that tends toward Grandeur. His diction is elevated and harsh to the point that it is almost stiff and austere. His style is abundant, but he does not use Distinctness, which is why he is often confusing and unclear. He is careful about word order and glories in balanced clauses (*parisōsis*). He does not use the kinds of style that reveal Character or Sincerity or any sort of Force except the kind that appears to be forceful but is not really.

Critias also uses a similar type. Thus we shall discuss him immediately after Antiphon the Sophist. His style is solemn in a way that is similar to Antiphon's, and it is elevated to produce loftiness. He often speaks categorically. His diction is purer than that of Antiphon, and when he uses Abundance he keeps his thoughts distinct. He often employs a sincere and persuasive style, especially in the proemia to his public speeches. Although his style is quite well wrought, he does not use ornamentation for its own sake or to excess or with obvious artifice, as Antiphon does. Instead he employs it in such a way that he seems sincere. He does not use very often any of the styles that reveal Character, such as Modesty or Simplicity or other such styles. This concludes our discussion of Critias. Next we shall discuss Lycurgus, who is also called Lycurgus the Orator, and this discussion ought naturally to follow that about Antiphon the Rhamnusian.

The style of Lycurgus is typical of practical oratory, except that he does not use the style that reveals Character through Simplicity; but his speeches have other qualities in addition to those that are associated with practical oratory. There is a lot of Asperity and Vehemence in his speeches, and these passages are not tempered by a well-wrought style. If they were, he would be indistinguishable from Dinarchus. But in his choice of diction the style of Lycurgus is much harsher, which is why I argue that it also possesses the kind of Force that seems to be forceful but is not really. For Lycurgus' speeches use commonplaces more than those of Dinarchus and sometimes use stronger invective in the handling

402

403 of the points that he makes. He often uses many digressions, indulging in myths, history, and poems, and this is also typical of the sort of Force that only appears to be forceful.

Andocides proposed to speak in a practical style, although he did not quite attain his goal. He is disjointed in his use of figures, and his style is not distinct. He uses many subordinate clauses. There is a lot of Abundance in his works because he uses parentheses, but the thought is often disordered because he does not employ Distinctness, which is why his style seems to some critics to be confused and generally unclear. There are very few of those elements that create a carefully wrought style and Beauty, and this is also true of Rapidity. There is a little, albeit a very little, of the sort of Force that depends on the approach, and almost none of the other kinds.

Thus the other ten orators, among whom I have included Critias, are inferior to Demosthenes. They carry off the second and third prizes in judicial and deliberative oratory. Since we now proceed to discuss pure panegyric oratory, we must deal with those writers who rank below Plato, just as before we discussed those that are inferior to Demosthenes.

Pure Panegyric (*Haplōs Panēgyrikos*)

12 It is not easy to say much about pure panegyric except that all those kinds of style out of which we said that the most beautiful panegyric style, which is that of Plato, is produced can be used individually in 404 great frequency to produce a kind of panegyric mode. That is, Solemnity can be used alone or Simplicity or Sweetness or Purity or a carefully wrought style, or any of the other styles that we discussed earlier, can be used simply. Those ancient authors who were famous for their panegyric oratory obviously used style in this way, and these are the authors whom we must now discuss.

First we must make some preliminary remarks. The most beautiful panegyric speech ought to possess Grandeur as well as charm, and also ornamentation and Clarity and realistic representations of people and all the other features of style that were discussed in our treatment of panegyric oratory. Not only poetry and prose in general exhibit these characteristics, but history possesses them all in abundance. Historians must surely be ranked among the panegyrists, as I think that they do engage in panegyrical writing, since they strive to create Grandeur and passages that give pleasure and almost all the other features that are typical of panegyric oratory, even though they are not as successful as Plato in this respect. So we must discuss them here too. But first we must deal with those writers who are famous for panegyric oratory but who rank below Plato, especially since some of them, such as Xenophon, whom we shall discuss first, wrote history as well as other sorts of prose.

Xenophon's style is very simple, and of those styles that are characteristic of panegyric oratory he uses Simplicity most frequently. He often employs the pleasures that are created by a simple style but uses   405 less often the sort of sweet passages that are produced by the narration of myths and other such topics. For example, when he discusses dogs in the *Cynegeticus* he creates pleasure by using an intensely simple style rather than by employing some other feature that is naturally characteristic of Sweetness. But all the Character depiction and emotion in the story of Abradates and Panthea in the *Cyropaideia* (7.3.8) is very pleasurable, because this is a tale of fiction told like a myth, which is also the case with the story of Tigranes and his wife Armenia (3.1.36). He rarely employs the sorts of Sweetness that are created by such passages, as we said, but they do sometimes appear in his works. His thoughts are often grand, but he tones them down, and by means of his approach, his diction, and those stylistic features that are related to the diction, he expresses them in a simple way. His style is as pure and distinct as that of any writer, but he does take delight in passages that are subtle and clever, whose qualities we discussed in our treatment of Sweetness and Simplicity. And his prose is very carefully wrought, as far, at least, as this is possible in a style that is basically simple and unaffected. In fact his style is much simpler than that of Plato, since the Simplicity is created by the subject matter itself as well as by the diction and those stylistic features that are related to the diction. Both authors, for example, wrote a *Symposium*. Xenophon does not hesitate to describe the entrances of dancers and certain kinds of dances and kisses and other similar aspects of a banquet, and he does it with charm. Plato, on the other hand, leaves such things to women, as he himself says (176e), and turns a basically simple event in a more solemn direc-   406 tion. Xenophon's historical works are similar to his other treatises, as is seen from the following passages from Book 4 of the *Anabasis*: "They wore crowns of straw" and "They talked to the children as if they were deaf and dumb" and "They had to drink bending over the bowl like cattle" (32–33). Such passages give pleasure because they are exceedingly simple. Plato does not employ this kind of Simplicity. Xenophon also does a marvelous job at depicting the characters in his works, especially when he represents people who are simple and truly unaffected and tender and pleasant, like Cyrus when he was still a boy and other similar characters. There is nothing like this in the works of Plato, except in the depiction of young boys, such as when he introduces Theaetetus or some similar character. But you could not really compare this with the depiction of Cyrus as a boy or the woman Armenia or other such characters in Xenophon. It is also typical of Xenophon to employ at intervals poetic words that are by nature very different from the diction that he normally uses, such as the verb *porsunein*, which means "to provide," and other such examples.

After Xenophon one would rank Aeschines the Socratic. His style is as simple as that of any writer, although Purity and Distinctness are really more typical of his prose than Simplicity. His diction is thus more graceful than that of Xenophon. He also employs quite a lot of thoughts that are rather solemn, and makes moderate use of passages that give pleasure because they deal with myths and fabulous stories. You could say in fact that Aeschines' style is more graceful than that of Xenophon to the same degree that Xenophon's style is simpler than that of Plato. His prose is much purer and even more carefully wrought than Xenophon's, at least as far as this is possible in a very simple style.

Nicostratus, who in my opinion, deserves, or perhaps demands, mention after Xenophon and Aeschines, uses a style that is no less simple than theirs, although it is more refined and much purer than that of almost any writer.[44] His style is plain (*hyperischnon*) and is never grand except, on occasion, in reference to the thought only. But he delights in myths and the pleasures that they give. In fact he himself has made up many of them. Some of these are like the fables of Aesop, but others could be made into plays. He is very meticulous about the arrangement (*syntaxis*) of the material in his works, but this does not detract from their Simplicity.

We have said enough about those writers who excelled in a certain kind of panegyric speech, among whom we included Nicostratus. Next we shall discuss outstanding historians. The *Olympic, Panathenaic,* and even *Panegyric Orations* of Isocrates and Lysias, despite their titles, obviously have a goal that is different from that of panegyric oratory. They have some characteristics that are typical of panegyric, but proba- 408 bly no more than a deliberative or judicial speech would admit. But even if they were of this type, which Isocrates' artistry in word order in particular might lead one to believe, what we have already said about them in our discussion of judicial and deliberative orators would still be sufficient. Now we must discuss historians other than Xenophon, whose works we dealt with earlier.

The most panegyrical of those historians who engage in panegyric is Herodotus. That is because his work is pure and distinct and very charming. Indeed he uses every sort of mythical thought and poetic language throughout his work. His thoughts are often grand. But it is a style that is carefully wrought and very artistic that gives his work both charm and Grandeur. Most of his rhythms, which are created by the word order and the clausulae, are dactylic and anapaestic and spondaic and, generally speaking, solemn. He depicts the Characters and emotions of those people whom he describes as beautifully and as poetically as any writer, and this is what often increases the Grandeur of a passage, especially in the discussion about human destiny between Xerxes and Artabanus in Book 7 (46–52). Here we conclude our discussion of Herodotus.

Before I discuss Thucydides I have to make one preliminary point. Although I mention him after Herodotus and the others, this does not 409 imply that I think that he is inferior to them in literary skill and talent. We would certainly not rank Herodotus after Nicostratus or Aeschines or even after Xenophon in literary talent and ability, especially since we are dealing here with the panegyric mode. We have simply followed a sequence determined by the manner in which we are discussing this type of style. In other words, we put the historians in a separate category from other writers who engaged in panegyric. And of the historians we discussed Herodotus first because he is more panegyrical and more charming, not only than Thucydides, but perhaps than any writer who engaged in panegyric. Some might have doubts as to where Thucydides should be treated. His style is typical of judicial and deliberative oratory as much as it is of panegyric. At least this is true of his thoughts and because he deals artistically with every point that he introduces. Let him be ranked where it is fitting, according to the kind of style that he uses and his superiority or inferiority to other writers in literary skill. We shall simply describe his style.

Thucydides aims especially at Grandeur, and he achieves it. But to me he does not seem to achieve the sort of Grandeur that he aims at. In my opinion, he wants his style to be solemn, which is typical of the kind of Grandeur that one finds in panegyric oratory. However, in his choice of diction and in the word order that he uses, he seems to me to go too far, which makes his style rough and austere and, consequently, unclear. He is very careful with his artistic adornment and obviously wants his style to be elevated and very weighty. But here again he goes too far in the use of hyperbole and novel kinds of word order, and this too tends to make his style austere and, consequently, unclear. Nevertheless his style is very dignified, and his thoughts are typical of practical oratory but are also solemn, which is a combination that one does not usually find. Not even in the narrative sections does he fail to treat his material artistically.[45]

His approaches, however, are not typical of practical oratory. He introduces even his artistic elaborations in a remarkably grand way or in a similar fashion, which is why his style is almost always without Sweetness. If he ever does produce a sweet passage, it appears to be very different from the type of style that he usually employs, as in the following example: "To Tereus, who took Procne the daughter of Pandion from Athens as his wife," etc. (2.29). There are other examples. Even if this were not the case, one should not be surprised that his style sometimes gives pleasure. Almost no style used by any individual author, even though he might choose to write in one particular kind of style and might even perfect it, could be considered pure and without some contact, at least, with all the other kinds of style.

Since he is a historian, Thucydides employs dramatic representation of character in the speeches and in some dialogues. But his style is the same even in those passages. The characteristics that we have attributed to him are even more remarkable here, since in the narrative his style is less austere and harsh. For in the narrative sections there are many

410

411

passages that are pure and distinct. In fact in this respect, as in many others, I think that he has surpassed his teacher Antiphon. Here we conclude our discussion of Thucydides.

Hecataeus of Miletus, from whom Herodotus learned much, is pure and clear, and in some passages also quite charming. He uses a pure, unmixed Ionic dialect, unlike the mixed variety that Herodotus uses, and this makes his diction less poetic. Nor is his style as carefully wrought or as embellished as that of Herodotus, which is why his works are much less charming, although almost his whole narration is composed of myths and similar kinds of stories. But his thought could lend itself to any kind of style, and his diction and those stylistic features that are related to diction, such as figures, clauses, word order, rhythms, and cadences, are well adapted to creating passages that are both charming and sweet, like those that one finds in Herodotus, as well as any other kind of passage, in fact, that the various types of style can naturally produce. One could thus reasonably assume that Hecataeus failed to produce such passages because he was not as concerned as Herodotus was with making his style carefully wrought and with the sort of embellishment that involves the diction. Here we conclude our discussion of Hecataeus.

It seems to be unnecessary to discuss Theopompus and Ephorus and 412
Hellanicus and Philistus and their like. First of all, given what we have already said about the various types of style and about individual writers, no one would have any difficulty in characterizing them. Secondly, the kinds of style that they used have, as far as I know, rarely or never been thought worthy of emulation or imitation by the Greeks, which is not the case with Thucydides, Herodotus, Hecataeus, Xenophon, and the other writers that I have discussed.

My next task would be to describe the poets who rank below Homer, just as we characterized the orators who rank below Demosthenes, and the prose writers who rank below Plato, by discussing Plato and Demosthenes first. We should probably follow the same procedure with Homer. But perhaps it was unnecessary for us to describe any individual authors. Those who have carefully studied these generic types of styles and the elements, as it were, out of which they are created—and this has been the subject of this whole treatise—ought to be able to characterize with ease any author, regardless of whether he is an ancient or a modern and whether he is a poet or a prose writer or an orator. So it would be superfluous to discuss each of the poets individually, and this would make our treatise very long. For before anyone could discuss that topic properly, he would have to say something about epic poetry and those

413 epic poets who rank second and third to Homer. And then he would have to discuss tragedy and comedy in a similar way, and then lyric poetry and all the other kinds, pointing out in each category who ranks first and second and why. The result would be that the discussion would go on almost indefinitely.[46]

Thus what we have already said must suffice, and our discussion *Concerning Types of Style* must end here. After this we will write the treatise *Concerning the Approach of Force*, which is, in a sense, an appendix to this treatise, although it is really much more important, as we pointed out earlier. But the treatise itself will make this clear.

Appendix I

Hermogenes and Ancient Critical Theories on Oratory

Hermogenes claims (215) to be dealing with types of style in an abstract way, and the use of the term *idea*, with its Platonic connotations, is meant to call attention to the pure and theoretical nature of his discussion. In fact the work is really a systematic analysis of the style of Demosthenes. It thus seems only fitting to compare and contrast it with other significant discussions of Demosthenic style in antiquity and to assess its value and analytic efficacy in comparison with them. The most significant of these discussions prior to Hermogenes' are the *Orator* of Cicero, written in 46 B.C., and the essay *On Demosthenes* in the critical essays of Dionysius of Halicarnassus, written sometime between 30 and 10 B.C., which may have been influenced by Cicero.[1]

Sometime between the publication of Cicero's *On the Orator* in 55 B.C. and the middle of the next decade the Neo-Atticist controversy had arisen in Rome. This was a stylistic debate that centered on the choice of proper oratorical models. The Neo-Atticists, led by Calvus, argued that the straightforward and relatively unadorned style of Lysias was the only suitable model for an orator to imitate. Cicero felt that this criticism was aimed at himself and the rather full and exuberant style that he had always used, and he wrote the *Orator* as a reply.[2] In it he argues that the style of Lysias is not the only Attic style and that the style of Demosthenes, which is much more varied, is consequently a much more suitable model for imitation. Hence the *Orator* contains a fairly extensive analysis of Demosthenes' style. Like Hermogenes, Cicero claims (7) to be dealing with style in an abstract way, and he does so to a greater extent than Hermogenes.

In his discussion Cicero uses the concept of the three styles—the plain, the middle, and the grand—which had probably been developed during the Hellenistic period, but which first appears in extant Latin literature in the *Rhetoric to Herennius*, written in the second decade of the first century B.C.[3] Cicero defines the three styles formally. The plain style (*Orat.* 75-90) is basically conversational. It avoids rhythm, periodic structure, and elaborate ornamentation and is not concerned about avoiding hiatus. The middle style (91–96) is smooth and ornamental. It uses metaphors and most of the figures of language, such as parallelism and antithesis. The grand style (97–99) is vigorous, powerful, and passionate. It uses figures of thought, such as rhetorical questions and exclamations.

In addition to this formal classification Cicero also defines the three styles functionally. Identifying each style with one of the *officia oratoris*, which are similar to the three modes of persuasion identified by Aristotle (*Rhet.* 1.2)—the logical, the ethical, and the pathetic—he argues (69) that the plain style should be used to instruct (*probare*), the middle to please and charm (*delectare*), and the grand to arouse the emotions (*flectere*). The secret of Demosthenes' style, according to Cicero, is his ability to use each of these three styles when and where it should be used. In fact, not only does he use all three styles, but he uses each of them more effectively than any other orator: "No one has ever excelled him either in the grand, the plain, or the middle style" (23).

Dionysius of Halicarnassus, whose essay is much more closely focused on the style of Demosthenes and less theoretical and abstract than either Cicero's or Hermogenes', uses the same critical system as Cicero and develops the same basic thesis, that Demosthenes' style is effective because he uses all three styles, the plain, the middle, and the grand, when and where they should be used. Dionysius' conception of what the three styles are, however, is somewhat different from that of Cicero and is, in my opinion, less clear since he defines the styles formally but not functionally. In the first part of his essay (*Dem.* 9) he defines the grand style, which he associates with Thucydides and Gorgias (8), neither of whom uses a style that is very moving, as the use of language and means of expression that are far removed from ordinary conversation. The plain style resembles the language of ordinary speech and is associated with the orator Lysias (2). The middle style is somewhere between the two extremes, not as artificial as that of Thucydides or Gorgias but less conversational than that of Lysias. This style Dionysius associates with Plato and Isocrates (3).

The secret of Demosthenes' style, according to Dionysius, is not only that he uses all three of these styles when and where they should be used but that he avoids the excesses and faults seen in Thucydides, Gorgias, Lysias, Isocrates, and Plato (34). His style is clearer than that of Thucydides and less artificial than that of Gorgias, more intense and emphatic than that of Lysias, and more varied and energetic than that of Plato and Isocrates.[4]

The most obvious advantage that Hermogenes' system has over Cicero's or Dionysius' is that it is considerably more subtle and hence more capable of bringing out various nuances of style that their systems do not pick up. Where they see three kinds of style he sees seven, four of which are divided into subtypes, producing a total of twenty. Admittedly these types could be grouped into clusters that correspond to the plain, the middle, and the grand.[5] But Hermogenes' system still conceptualizes and classifies several varieties of these three types of style that do not exist in Cicero and Dionysius.

Secondly, in keeping with the greater subtlety of his system, Hermogenes usually thinks in terms of small units, short passages or sentences, rather than speeches or large sections of speeches. Cicero, although he argues that various parts of a speech must be written in different styles (*Orat.* 74), seems to think more in terms of whole speeches when he actually gives examples of the various styles (102–103, 110–111). Dionysius also generally gives very long examples.

Thirdly, Hermogenes, more so than either Cicero or Dionysius, quite rightly lays a lot of emphasis on the role of content (*ennoia*) in determining what stylistic effect a passage produces. In other words, he sees style in a much less purely formal way than they do. Cicero does argue (72) that certain topics require a particular style, that the grandeur and majesty of the Roman people, for example, should not be discussed in the plain style; but he sees this more as a question of style being appropriate to content than of content contributing to stylistic effect. Dionysius' analysis is completely formal. Hermogenes, on the other hand, looks on content as the very basis of stylistic effect, which is why in his analysis of each of the types of style he always discusses *ennoia* first.

Finally, another advantage that Hermogenes has, not only over Cicero and Dionysius but over every other ancient critic, is that he discusses both what a particular figure of speech is called and also what function or effect it has in the speech or in the particular passage in which it appears—in other words, how form reflects content (cf. 290–291).

But the best way to examine the efficacy of Hermogenes' system is by seeing how well it can be used to explicate a passage of Demosthenes. I have chosen, somewhat at random, *Philippic* I. 34–35, of which I offer the following translation:

(1) Then what in addition to this? (2) You yourselves will be free from harm, not as before, when, having made an attack against Lemnos and Imbros, Philip went away, having your fellow citizens as prisoners of war; having stopped the grain ships at Geraestus he levied untold sums; finally he landed at Marathon and left the land, having the sacred trireme: but you are able neither to prevent these acts nor, at the times which you propose, to send aid. (3) And yet why in the world, gentlemen of Athens, do you think that the Panathenaic and Dionysiac festivals always take place at the appropriate time—whether professionals or private individuals are chosen to be in charge of them, for which festivals so much money is spent as is not spent for even one of the military expeditions (and they involve as many people and as much preparation as anything in the world does, as far as I know)—but all your expeditions are too late for the crisis, the one to Methone, the one to Pagasae, the one to Potidaea?

Demosthenes then proceeds to answer the question that he has just posed.

I suppose that Cicero and Dionysius would both say that the first two sentences of this passage illustrate the plain style. The structure of the clauses is very simple. The vocabulary is conversational. There is very little subordination except in the use of participles. The section is basically narrative. However, these sentences do much more than simply narrate facts in the plain style, as is revealed by applying the stylistic criteria of Hermogenes.

The first sentence, for example, tends to make the passage distinct, as a question which is then answered always does (239). And it is especially important that this section be distinct since it contains what is really the most important idea in the speech.

Likewise, in the second sentence the short clauses at the beginning, filled with verbs and participles and having no connectives between them, create an effect that Hermogenes calls Rapidity (312). Another hallmark of Rapidity is that all these clauses express particular examples of the same phenomenon, Philip's aggressions against Athens (316).

Moreover, there is no hiatus in the first part of the sentence; and, as Hermogenes points out (319), the avoidance of hiatus makes the style quick and rapid. Also, although Cicero (*Orat.* 77) and Dionysius (*Lys.* 3) both argue that metrical effects are not used in the plain style, the predominant meter used in the first part of this sentence is trochaic, which Hermogenes associates with a rapid style (319). The second instance cited of Philip's aggression against Athens, for example, ends with the words *amȳthēía chrēmat' exelexe* ("he levied untold sums"), which is clearly a trochaic rhythm. In addition, the two parts of the next clause end in a rhythmical pattern that is very similar to the one that Hermogenes himself gives as an example of a trochaic pattern from Demosthenes (320), although this is not as clear-cut as the one cited above: *eis Marathōn' apebē* ("he landed at Marathon") and *oíchet' echon triērē* ("he left, having the sacred trireme"). So, using Hermogenes' system, one would characterize this part of the sentence as being "rapid." Rapidity is quite appropriate here since Demosthenes wants to emphasize Philip's energy and activity. In other words, style reflects content.

In the last part of the second sentence, however, which describes the lethargy and lack of activity of the Athenians, the style becomes slow. The use of negative polysyndeton ("neither . . . nor") and synonymity, since both of these clauses really say the same thing, creates an effect that Hermogenes would call Abundance (284–286). The rhythm of this part of the sentence contains more long syllables than the first part (for example, *kōluein eis toùs chronoûs*, "to prevent at the times"), and this too slows down the speed of the passage. The insertion of the subordinate clause "which you propose" before the infinitive "to send aid," which completes the meaning of the main clause, also creates an abundant and halting effect, as Hermogenes points out (288). Altogether this is quite an apt way to convey the slowness, apathy, and indifference of the Athenians.

Now let us consider the sentence as a whole. In the first part Demosthenes wants to call attention to Philip's successes in order to arouse his audience to action; but he does not want to dwell upon them so much that he will discourage the Athenians. "Rapidity" is an admirable style to accomplish this purpose. In the last part of the sentence he does want to dwell upon the fact that Athens' real problems stem from her own lack of activity; this is exactly the effect that Abundance produces. Moreover, in this sentence, which reflects the antithesis, seen throughout the entire speech, between Philip's energy and activity and the Athenians' lethargy, he has mixed two styles that are very different, one that is energetic and quick and another that is slow and lingering. It is this mixture, even in the same sentence, of opposing styles that, as Hermogenes rightly points out (279), gives Demosthenes' speeches that variety that is their hallmark.

The third sentence is periodic. Presumably both Cicero and Dionysius would consequently see it as an example of the middle style, although its purpose is hardly to please—which Cicero, at least, sees as the function of the middle style. In Hermogenes' terms, the style here is also "abundant," and again this is a more enlightening term than "middle." Many aspects of this sentence are characteristic of Abundance. First, many details are given, which breaks the general statement down into its component parts (279). Secondly, there is the long parenthesis, "whether professionals or private individuals are chosen to be in charge of them . . ."; as Hermogenes points out (294), parentheses, which delay the completion of the thought by adding extraneous comments, produce Abundance. Thirdly, the sentence uses a lot of subordination, which also creates Abundance (288). And finally, the full expression of ideas—"so much money is spent as is not spent" and "as many people and as much preparation as anything in the world does, as far as I know"—which Hermogenes calls hypostasis (290), also makes the style abundant.

Abundance is again quite appropriate here, since this sentence describes the copiousness of preparations that are made for festivals. In the last part of the third sentence, however, the style once again becomes rapid, with the short phrases at the end, the asyndeton, and the anaphora in "the one to Methone, the one to Pagasae, the one to Potidaea" (316); and the meter of the beginning of this clause is trochaic, $\overline{tous}$ d' $\overline{apos}\breve{to}l\overline{ous}$ ("but the expeditions"). This contrast between the fullness of preparations for public festivals and the short shrift that is given to military expeditions is thus reflected in the Abundance of the style that states the former, which takes up about seventy percent of the sentence, and the brevity of the style that depicts the latter.

Moreover, this whole sentence is a question that is then immediately answered. And this, like the question in the first sentence, creates Distinctness, which is so important in this passage.

From this single example one sees that Hermogenes' system can bring
out stylistic effects that are closely related to the content of the passage,
effects that the systems of Cicero and Dionysius do not reveal. Anyone
who has read Hermogenes carefully and who knows the speeches of
Demosthenes will see countless other passages that will repay similar
analysis.

Appendix 2

Hermogenes on Panegyric

Most of Hermogenes' treatise is very precise and very clearly focused on oratory, specifically on what is often called "primary" rhetoric.[1] In other words, Hermogenes is concerned with what effect an orally delivered speech would have had on the audience before which it was delivered. At the end, however, when he begins to discuss panegyric (in "Practical Oratory"), his conception of what sort of material is appropriate for rhetorical criticism becomes much broader.

Hermogenes first discusses what he calls the "panegyric style in prose" (387) and gives as the most beautiful example of it the style of Plato. This, he says, is similar to deliberative and judicial oratory, which he has already discussed under "purely" practical or political speeches (*logoi haplōs politikoi*, 384–387), except that it shows a predominance of those types that create Grandeur (except Asperity and Vehemence which for obvious reasons are not appropriate in panegyric), Simplicity, and those types that make the style sweet, carefully wrought, pretty, and charming. The style should be forceful, but not apparently so; and since most panegyric is narrative there should be some Rapidity (387). Panegyric passages in a speech delivered in a real case, however, should be constructed out of the types that are suitable for deliberative oratory: Grandeur, the sort of Force that both is and seems to be forceful, and Character, except that Brilliance and Solemnity should be used more often than in a purely deliberative speech. In other words, quite in keeping with the emphasis on primary rhetoric in the rest of the work, Hermogenes is here discussing passages with panegyric overtones in deliberative and judicial oratory, in addition to the philosophical works of Plato, which he sees as being more basically panegyric in nature. The emphasis, however, is still on rhetoric as "an art of persuasion."[2]

The beginning of the first paragraph at 389, however, is rather startling: "All poetry is panegyric and is, in fact, the most panegyric of all literary styles. Therefore, we must discuss what is the most effective kind of poetry as we discussed what is the most effective kind of panegyric." Then Hermogenes seems to veer off in an even more radically different direction. Homer, he says, (echoing Aristotle), is the best of poets: since poetry is an imitation of all things, the man who best imitates *orators* who deliver speeches and *singers* who sing panegyrics is also the best of orators and speech-writers (389–390).

At 391 he backs away from this extremely broad discussion and returns to his treatment of panegyric. The most admirable panegyric speech, he argues, is created not only from the types of style that he has already associated with panegyric, but also from the stylistic features that are usually associated with poetry, although these elements, especially the use of meter, are not as obvious as they would be in poetry. He then proceeds to outline these features: mythical stories, dwelling upon details, invocation of the Muses, and meter (391–395).

In a very real sense Hermogenes is simply repeating himself here, since he has already associated the features that he sees as being typical of poetry with those types of style that are sweet, carefully wrought, pretty, and charming. And he has already said (387) that these traits are characteristic of panegyric. Nevertheless the scope of his discussion has become broader, for at the end of this treatment of panegyric (395) he names Homer and Plato as the representatives of the most beautiful kind of panegyric. Neither, however, was what we normally consider a practicing orator.

Then Hermogenes backtracks somewhat and discusses (395–403) the style of "practical orators" (395) who rank below Demosthenes—the other members of the "canon" of Attic orators plus Critias, all of whom were engaged in what is called primary rhetoric. Then, in accordance with this scheme, he proposes (404) to discuss writers of panegyric who rank below Plato. Here again the scope of his treatment becomes much broader than before:

Not only poetry and prose in general exhibit these characteristics [of a panegyric speech], but history possesses them all in abundance. Historians must surely be ranked among the panegyrists, as I think that they do engage in panegyrical writing, since they strive to create Grandeur and passages that give pleasure and almost all the other features that are typical of panegyric oratory, even though they are not as successful as Plato in this respect. So we must discuss them here too.

He then proceeds to discuss Xenophon; Aeschines the Socratic, who wrote philosophical dialogues; Nicostratus, who wrote fables; Herodotus, "the most panegyrical of those historians who engage in panegyric" (408); Thucydides; and Hecataeus of Miletus, who wrote ethnographical works (404–412). He also mentions Theopompus, Ephorus, Hellanicus, and Philistus, who were historians (412), but he does not discuss them in any detail.

Interestingly, however, he excludes from consideration the *Olympic Oration* of Lysias and the *Panathenaic* and *Panegyric Orations* of Isocrates, speeches that are usually classified as panegyric oratory. He argues that although these speeches have some characteristics that are typical of panegyric, they probably have no more than any judicial or deliberative speech normally would. In other words, he seems to be excluding from panegyric those speeches that were or purport to have been delivered before actual audiences on specific occasions and to be relegating all such speeches and all practicing orators to the rubric of deliberative or judicial oratory. He reserves the term "panegyric" for those kinds of literature that have certain rhetorical features but that are not what we normally consider oratory. Evidently he regarded deliberative and judicial oratory as a concern of primary rhetoric; panegyric seems to be an aspect of "secondary" rhetoric.[3] Thus panegyric seems in Hermogenes' work to have undergone a process of *letteraturizzazione*: "the tendency of rhetoric to shift its focus from persuasion to narration, from civic to personal texts, and from discourse to literature, including poetry."[4]

This is corroborated by the end of the work. Here Hermogenes says (412) that the next task in his treatment of panegyric would be to discuss all the poets, epic, lyric, tragic, and comic, who rank below Homer. But he breaks off and concludes the work quickly, since that projected task would make his discussion go on "almost indefinitely."

It thus seems clear that in Hermogenes' system panegyric has passed from primary to secondary rhetoric. This is a tendency of all rhetorical systems and was especially pronounced in the ancient world under the Roman empire because of the limited possibilities for the practice of deliberative and judicial oratory. It can also be seen in the treatise *On the Sublime*, (the date of which is unknown, but which may be contemporary with Hermogenes), and earlier in the works of Dionysius of Halicarnassus and Demetrius.[5] Hermogenes' conception of panegyric therefore seems to be the natural conclusion of a tendency that had been developing in Greek rhetoric for centuries.

Notes

INTRODUCTION

1. When I use these terms in the translation, or adjectives derived from them, I am using them in a technical sense. See also n. 1 to Book 1.
2. See n.2 to Book 1.
3. Patterson, *Hermogenes and the Renaissance*, 186.
4. Ibid., 33.
5. For a discussion of how the system can be used to explain Demosthenes' style, with examples from the orator in translation, see Wooten, *Cicero's Philippics*, 21–42.
6. Kennedy, *Art of Rhetoric*, 349.
7. Ibid., 629.
8. See Kennedy, *Greek Rhetoric*, 96–101.

BOOK I

1. Throughout the translation I have used the word *type* where Hermogenes uses the technical term *idea*. At times it has seemed to me appropriate to insert some explanatory material into the text itself or to expand what Hermogenes says rather than referring the reader to a footnote. I have indicated these inclusions of my own with square brackets.
2. *Methodos*, which I have translated "approach to the thought," involves primarily the manner of treating the subject matter—directly, for example, as opposed to allusively. Later in the work it is related closely to figures of thought, since they also involve a way of approaching the major theme. *Lexis*, which I have here translated "style," is later used more in the sense of "diction," a major component, of course, of style. For a discussion of these terms see Kennedy, *Greek Rhetoric*, 97–98.
3. *Anapausis*, which I have here translated "cadence" and in the next sentence "pause," which is its basic meaning, is the metrical configuration that indicates the major pauses or stops in the sentence—what in Latin is called a *clausula*.
4. Hermogenes here uses language that is more appropriate to a discussion of style in reference to building, and I have translated the terms in keeping with that image. Word order (*synthēkē*) is the "manner of putting the building materials together," and "restrictions placed on how they are put together" corresponds to cadence (*anapausis*), since the cadence that is being used to mark major pauses in the sentence imposes certain restrictions on how the words can be arranged.
5. Hermogenes discusses later what topics are characteristic of Brilliance.
6. In the Greek construction, a genitive absolute, the noun is in the genitive case.

7. Hermogenes is here talking about the speech *Against Aristocrates*. Charidemus of Oreus was a mercenary who was in the employ of Cersobleptes, king of Thrace. The policy of Eubulus, Demosthenes' political opponent at this time, was to maintain an alliance with Cersobleptes and to keep him strong so that Thrace would be a buffer state between Macedonia, in the west, and the Athenian possessions in the Thracian Chersonese to the east. Demosthenes' policy was to keep Cersobleptes, who was involved in a civil war in his own kingdom, weak by stirring up trouble in Thrace and to distract Philip by attacking him elsewhere. Demosthenes realized that Cersobleptes could threaten the Athenian colonies in the Chersonese as easily as Philip and objected to the Athenian policy of using someone else to protect Athens' own possessions.

8. *Emphasis* is a means of expression by which the orator means more than he seems to say; see Kennedy, *Greek Rhetoric*, 94, 286, 309-310. A "figured problem" is a rhetorical exercise in which the speaker's real purpose is quite different from what it appears to be, especially when he seems to be arguing against himself, although his real purpose is to praise himself. Thus it is a case that lends itself to ironic treatment. See Kennedy, *Greek Rhetoric*, 93-94, and Russell, *Greek Declamation*, 35-37.

9. The *Deliacus* was a speech delivered by Hyperides soon after 343 B.C., in which he argued for Athens' right to the presidency of the temple of Apollo on Delos. In the speech he evidently recounted the story of Leto in a very poetical way. The speech was admired by Longinus (*On the Sublime* 34).

10. In this passage Herodotus is discussing why the Nile rises in the summer.

11. In 406 B.C., toward the end of the Peloponnesian War, the Athenian fleet defeated the Spartans and their allies at the battle of Arginusae. However, a storm arose soon after the battle had begun, and the Athenians consequently were unable to rescue sailors who had been shipwrecked. The casualties from the battle were therefore enormous. Feeling in Athens against the generals, who were thought to have been negligent, was hostile; and in what was probably an illegal move, six of them were condemned to death en masse. The speech to which Hermogenes refers was not an actual speech of the time but a work of the sophist Aelius Aristides composed in the second century A.D. It is not extant.

12. In Book 8 (65) Herodotus tells the story that after Attica had been abandoned by the Athenians a man named Dicaeus thought that he heard thousands of Athenians marching from Eleusis to Athens shouting "Iacchus," a cry that was associated with the mysteries of Demeter celebrated at Eleusis.

13. According to Longinus (*On the Sublime* 3.2), Gorgias provoked laughter among his audience by using this image.

14. In his comment on this passage Syrianus (ed. Rabe, 47-48) tells us that a "mixed trochaic" verse is composed of iambs and trochees.

15. We are not sure about the source of this quotation. Dionysius of Halicarnassus quotes it in the treatise *On Composition* (23-24) and says that it comes from the *Sotadeia*, which may mean simply from the works of Sotades, a comic poet

of the third century B.C. Cf. Demetrius *On Style* 189. The meter is a form of ionics used by Sotades, often called the Sotadean, which does not break down into readily recognizable feet; cf. Maas, *Greek Metre*, 27.

16. In his comment on this passage Syrianus says (ed. Rabe, 50) that words that contain harsh sounds or conjunctions of sounds that grate on the ear are "harsh in themselves," and that is surely what Hermogenes is discussing in the second half of this paragraph. Syrianus gives as an additional example the word *dardaptōn*.

17. In the speech *On the Chersonese* (74), from which this sentence comes, Demosthenes is quoting the general Timotheus, who spoke urging the Athenians to make an expedition to Euboea in 357, as an example of how Athenians should act.

18. Hermogenes is here referring to the *progymnasmata*, preliminary exercises in rhetorical composition, in which students were asked to write passages of certain sorts. One of the exercises, called "the commonplace," was a passage attacking vice. See Kennedy, *Greek Rhetoric*, 54-73, especially 62-63. Oration 25, which Hermogenes cites, is actually not by Demosthenes.

19. "Aristides" (Walz, *Rhetores Graeci*, 9:346) defines *apostasis* as occurring when we "abandon the combination and conjunction of thoughts in sequence and go back to a fresh start." He gives examples, and these support the translation of *apostasis* as "a fresh start."

20. Syrianus says (ed. Rabe, 53) that it is the length of the clauses, which are rather long instead of short, as they would be in a harsh passage, that makes this sentence more brilliant than harsh. In fact in his comment on this passage he succinctly outlines the relationship between Florescence and the other types that Hermogenes discusses. In thought and approach it is like Asperity and Vehemence. In diction it is like Asperity, Vehemence, and Brilliance. In figures it is like Vehemence and Brilliance. In composition—clauses, word order, cadences, and rhythm—it is like Brilliance. Thus this type is really created out of elements that are characteristic of other types.

21. In other words, here Demosthenes prefaces the statement "The Olynthians would have many things to say" with an example of what they *could* say; and thus we do not expect this to follow. When the passage is quoted above, however, Hermogenes omits this little dialogue that precedes the statement and thus casts the passage in such a way that we expect an example to follow.

22. In his comment Syrianus tries (ed. Rabe, 54) to clarify this rather confusing passage. He says, in reference to the two sentences quoted by Hermogenes, that the thought of the one about Euboea, which is directed at Philip, is harsh and that the one about Lasthenes, which concerns traitors, is vehement. However, these two thoughts also have an element of Brilliance, because Demosthenes is very confident about what he is saying. The approach of the sentences is typical of Brilliance, since the thoughts are introduced in a direct way without interruption. The figures are also characteristic of Brilliance: the sentences produce a cumulative effect. They do not use figurative language, and the long clauses are

also typical of Brilliance. However, one could not properly say that in these two sentences we have simply a mixture of Asperity or Vehemence and Brilliance, which would create Florescence. The thoughts are not sufficiently reproachful to be called truly harsh or vehement, and there is an element of Brilliance even in the thought. That is why Hermogenes argues that these sentences exemplify Brilliance and Florescence.

23. As Syrianus points out (ed. Rabe, 57–58), Aristotle discusses these in Book 2 of the *Rhetoric* (18–19).

24. I cannot find any passages where other critics, such as Dionysius of Halicarnassus or the writers of the scholia to Demosthenes, discuss these particular sentences as being examples of Abundance.

25. See note 8 above.

26. Cf. Quintilian 5.10.95.

27. Syrianus says (ed. Rabe, 58) that Abundance is created in the thought because Demosthenes not only narrates the facts but also introduces the people involved and the reasons why certain events took place. In the approach, he introduces reasons for making a statement before making the statement itself, which is also typical of Abundance.

28. According to Syrianus (ed. Rabe, 58), the second phrase is generic (*genos*) while the first is specific (*eidos*), and to relate the general as well as the particular is a thought that is typical of Abundance.

29. Syrianus says (ed. Rabe, 58–59) that Brilliance could not be used in the private speeches, since in them Demosthenes is not dealing with noble deeds. Asperity would be inappropriate, since he is not reproaching those who are more powerful than himself. For the same reason, Florescence could not be used. The Vehemence of certain passages is toned down since one private citizen does not usually direct at another the kinds of fierce reproaches that Demosthenes, for example, directs at Aeschines in the speech *On the Crown*.

30. Syrianus comments (ed. Rabe, 59–60) that even in public speeches there are not many passages in which an orator discusses elevated topics in a solemn style and that an orator must avoid making too many criticisms, which would use Asperity, Vehemence, or Florescence, so that he will not appear to be carping, which would undermine his ethical appeal.

31. I have here expanded Hermogenes' explanation somewhat, in accordance with the discussion of this passage in Syrianus (ed. Rabe, 62–63).

32. Dionysius of Halicarnassus uses *chrōma* in this sense (*Letter to Ammaeus* 2.2).

33. See the very good discussion of this aspect of Demosthenes' style in Rowe, "Demosthenes' Use of Language," 182–192.

34. In the Greek the three phrases that make up this sentence end in the same sound, producing a rhyming effect: *tei te polei boēthein ōietai dein kai dikēn hyper hautou labein, touto kāgō peirāsomai poiein.*

35. I do not know the source of this discussion, but Syrianus tells us (ed. Rabe, 64) that the reason was that Androtion was a pupil of Isocrates.

36. The Greek example involves homoioteleuton and homoioptoton, in addition to parallelism, since the last word in each phrase ends in the same sound (*-kota*) and is in the same case, the accusative. The Greek is not awkward.

37. It is easier to see Hermogenes' point in the Greek: *to labein oun ta didomena homologōn ennomon einai, to charin toutōn apodounai paranomōn graphei.*

38. In his final comment Hermogenes is really talking about assonance and homoioteleuton, although he continues to use the general term for parallelism, *parisōsis*, which usually refers to balance throughout the clause.

39. Adjectives describing the human body were the source of much critical stylistic terminology in the ancient world.

40. This figure is usually called litotes.

41. Once again I do not know the source of this discussion.

42. Syrianus says (ed. Rabe, 67–68) that those feet are related to one another and are mutually compatible that take the same amount of time to pronounce, such as spondees ($-\,-$) and dactyls ($-\,\smile\,\smile$).

43. Hermogenes says in his discussion of Solemnity (253–254) that stately cadences are produced when the clause ends in a word of three or more syllables that itself ends in a long syllable.

44. *Bebēkōs*, which I have translated "stately," is the perfect participle of the verb *bainō*, whose basic meaning is "to walk, to stand, or to be firmly poised." Its opposite is *kremamenos*, which I have translated "to be suspended." The image is probably related to walking, a forceful, majestic gait (*bebēkōs*) as opposed to one that is halting and limps (*kremamenos*).

45. This is a reference to Dionysius of Halicarnassus' *On Composition* (17; and see the note in Syrianus, ed. Rabe, 69). Dionysius does not consider the diphthong *ei* an appropriate long sound for a stately rhythm.

BOOK 2

1. See Spengel, *Rhetores Graeci*, 3:139.

2. Hermogenes here contrasts figures that are necessarily (*kat' anankēn*) concise with those that he discussed earlier (314–315) that are naturally (*physei*) concise.

3. Demetrius *On Style* (268) and Dionysius of Halicarnassus *On Composition* (9) both discuss this famous passage from Aeschines.

4. A *symplokē* is technically a combination of anaphora and antistrophe, as in the example given from Aeschines, although Hermogenes uses the term loosely here to refer to any *x . . . y* / *x . . . y* combination or to a chiasmus. See Lausberg, *Handbuch*, no. 633.

5. Syrianus (ed. Rabe, 71) says that such a sentence appears to be concise because the speaker passes quickly from one topic to another and that it seems to be rapid because the clauses are short. But it is really abundant, because many thoughts are involved in a single concept that is broken down into its component parts.

6. Cf. the discussion in Demetrius *On Style* (20), where the author uses a similar terminology.

7. As Syrianus points out (ed. Rabe, 71–72), the whole passage must be quoted to see what Hermogenes means here: "The one who was annexing Euboea and making it a base of operations against Attica and attacking Megara and occupying Oreus and destroying Porthmus and setting up Philistides as tyrant in Oreus and Cleitarchus in Eretria and putting the Hellespont under his control and besieging Byzantium and destroying some Greek cities and restoring exiles in others, by doing these things was he acting unjustly and breaking the treaty and violating the terms of peace or not?" In the main clause "breaking the treaty" and "violating the terms of peace" are specific examples (*eidē*) of a general class (*genos*), which is "acting unjustly." Euboea is a whole, of which Oreus and Porthmus are parts. "Some Greek cities" is undefined, but Byzantium, Oreus, and Eretria are defined.

8. Hermogenes is discussing here the kind of character portrayal (*ēthopoiia*) that is generally associated with the speeches of Lysias; cf. Kennedy, *The Art of Persuasion*, 135–136 and Aristotle *Rhetoric* 1.2.4.

9. Our texts of Demosthenes must derive from those produced by scholars who deleted the passage.

10. Demosthenes' speech *On the Crown* is technically a private speech, but one that obviously had to deal with momentous issues.

11. See note 9 above.

12. I can not identify these critics.

13. Syrianus says (ed. Rabe, 77) that these words sound rough and hard because of the conjunction of consonants that clash (*pt* and *nk*). This is typical of the style that Hermogenes calls Asperity, which is a subtype of Grandeur.

14. Syrianus says (ed. Rabe, 77) that this description appeals to the sight, which Hermogenes has mentioned earlier as a typical source of this kind of pleasure.

15. In the next passage (241e) Socrates makes reference to his having broken into verse.

16. The word *atreēs* also means "not to be feared."

17. In 357 the Athenians had granted citizenship to the mercenary general Charidemus of Oreus. Four years later a decree was proposed that the person of Charidemus should be inviolable, that is, that anyone who killed him could be summarily arrested and that relations between Athens and any state that harbored his murderer would be broken. Demosthenes wrote this speech for a man named Euthycles, who brought a charge of illegality against the decree. In it he argues that the special decree is unconstitutional if Charidemus is really an Athenian citizen (20–100).

18. By "deliberative speeches" Hermogenes means the early deliberative speeches, those that are sometimes referred to as the Hellenic Orations: *For the Megalopolitans*, *On the Symmories*, and *On the Freedom of the Rhodians*, in contrast to the *Philippics*.

19. The prayer at the beginning of the speech *On the Crown* asks the Athenians for their goodwill, which indicates that there was some fear on Demosthenes' part about how his speech would be received. The speech to which Hermogenes refers is Aelius Aristides' *Sicilian Oration* 1.40 (ed. Dindorf, 1:567). Aelius Aristides and Nicostratus are the only orators later than the fourth century B.C. that Hermogenes cites as classic models.

20. This discussion is not now extant. It seems likely that Hermogenes lectured on Demosthenes' speeches, and that is probably the discussion to which he is now referring.

21. Syrianus (ed. Rabe, 81–82) gives as an example of a formal introduction (*katastasis*) "I know that my opponent will rely especially on this argument."

22. Syrianus says (ed. Rabe, 82) that this would have been formally presented (*katastatikōs*) if Demosthenes had said: "As is accustomed to happen in the case of a ship and those sailing on it, while the ship is safe," etc.

23. As Syrianus points out (ed. Rabe, 83–84), not to give the second half of a division is tantamount to saying that the first half is so obvious that the alternative should not even be expressed.

24. As in the preceding example, this sentence is introduced by the particle *men*, "on the one hand," which would lead one to expect a contrasting sentence introduced by *de*, "on the other." But this is not given.

25. On the authenticity of these letters see Goldstein, *The Letters of Demosthenes*, 3–34.

26. Batalus was the nickname that Demosthenes' nurse gave him (Aeschin. 1.126). Its basic meaning is "stammerer," but Aeschines tries to give it an opprobrious connotation. Oenomaus was a hero of Greek tragedy who was celebrated in a play of Sophocles in which Aeschines had acted.

27. See n. 8 to Book 1. This particular type of exercise is called a *prosangelia*, a speech in which a man argues that his life is worthless and should be ended. See Russell, *Greek Declamation*, 35–37.

28. The life of Themistocles was a popular topic in declamation. See Russell, *Greek Declamation*, 114–118.

29. According to Demosthenes (18.204), Cyrsilus had advised the Athenians to surrender to Xerxes. Herodotus gives his name as Lycidas (9.5).

30. There seems to be an echo here, and elsewhere, of Aeschylus' *Seven Against Thebes* 592: "He wants not to seem to be the bravest, but to be."

31. According to Syrianus (ed. Rabe, 87), not giving advance notice of his amazement is an approach that is typical of Sincerity. The use of direct address is characteristic of Vehemence, and the balanced clauses and homoioteleuton create Beauty.

32. Lysias' oratory has often been called a good example of "the art that conceals art." See Jebb, *The Attic Orators*, 1:170.

33. See Hagedorn, *Zur Ideenlehre des Hermogenes*, 84–85, for a discussion of this passage and its implications. His argument is that Hermogenes was so over-

whelmed at the thought of the enormity of the task, as he indicates in the next passage, that he never wrote the separate work that he here envisions. The work that has come down to us under the title *On the Approach of Force*, as Hagedorn points out, is not by Hermogenes.

34. Hermogenes is talking about what are generally referred to as the "attributes of a case"; cf. Cicero *On Invention* 1.38.

35. Cf. the discussion in Plato *Ion* 536e–542b.

36. The most representative of Hermogenes' conception of panegyric, with its mythical and Platonic associations, at least among extant writers, are the works of Himerius in the fourth century A.D. Surviving mythological speeches by Gorgias, Isocrates, and others are not treated in this poetic way. But there must have been a tradition of some sort. The *Eroticus* attributed to Demosthenes might be an example of it.

37. Cf. Dio Chrysostom *The First Discourse on Kingship* 10.

38. I cannot find the source for this statement.

39. This characterization is somewhat surprising given the fullness of argument that one finds in the speeches of Isaeus; cf. Kennedy, *Art of Persuasion*, 145.

40. These words appear only in quotations of Hyperides in other authors; see fragments 34, 78, and 239 (taken from Hermogenes), ed. Jensen.

41. I do not know who these critics were, although Dionysius of Halicarnassus has the same general opinion of Dinarchus (*On Dinarchus* 5).

42. Hermogenes may be thinking of the discussion in Plato *Menex.* 236a, which could be interpreted as seeing Antiphon the Rhamnusian and Antiphon the sophist as the same person. In any case, whether Antiphon the orator and Antiphon the sophist were one or two persons remains a subject of speculation. See Morrison, "Antiphon."

43. For a discussion of the "canon" of the ten Attic orators see Kennedy, *Art of Persuasion*, 125.

44. Nicostratus was a sophist and a philosopher who was more or less contemporaneous with Hermogenes. He and Aelius Aristides are the only nonclassical writers whom Hermogenes discusses. None of his works are extant. Hermogenes may have known him, and this reference may have been a personal tribute.

45. Hermogenes' discussion of Thucydides is reminiscent of the essay *On the Style of Thucydides* by Dionysius of Halicarnassus and may have been inspired by it.

46. Dionysius of Halicarnassus did this in the treatise *On Imitation*; and cf. Kennedy, *Art of Rhetoric*, 346–350. A similar discussion can be found at the beginning of Book 10 of Quintilian.

APPENDIX I

1. Cf. Kennedy, *Art of Rhetoric*, 342–353.
2. Ibid., 241–259.

3. Ibid., 70-71.
4. In the second half of the essay Dionysius makes a separate division based specifically on composition, that is, how words are put together into sentences. Here too he sees Demosthenes as exemplifying a blend of the "rugged" harmony found in Thucydides and the "smooth" harmony found in Plato. See Kennedy, *Art of Rhetoric*, 359-360.
5. Clarity, Character, and Sincerity, including their subtypes, could fall under the rubric of the plain style in the classifications of both Dionysius and Cicero. Rapidity, based on a purely formal classification, would also probably be classified there. If we assume, as Cicero does, that the purpose of the middle style is to please, we should classify three subtypes of Grandeur—Solemnity, Brilliance, and Abundance—under that rubric. That would leave the other subtypes of Grandeur—Asperity, Vehemence, and Florescence—under the grand style, whose purpose is to arouse the emotions. Under Dionysius' system one might be tempted to put Beauty under the rubric of the grand style. It does not arouse emotion, but like Asperity, Vehemence, and Florescence, it is far removed from the language of everyday life, as is Rapidity to a certain extent.

APPENDIX 2

1. Kennedy, *Classical Rhetoric*, 4.
2. Ibid.
3. Ibid., 5.
4. Ibid.
5. Ibid., 112-114.

Bibliography

Baldwin, Charles Sears. *Medieval Rhetoric and Poetic*. New York: Macmillan, 1928.

Chaignet, Anthelme Edouard. *La rhétorique et son histoire*. Paris: E. Bouillon & E. Vieweg, 1888.

Dindorf, Wilhelm, ed. *Aristides*. 3 vols. Leipzig, 1829. Reprinted Hildesheim: Georg Olms, 1964.

Goldstein, Jonathan. *The Letters of Demosthenes*. New York: Columbia University Press, 1968.

Hagedorn, Dieter. *Zur Ideenlehre des Hermogenes*. Göttingen: Vandenhoeck & Ruprecht, 1964.

Jebb, Richard. *The Attic Orators from Antiphon to Isaeus*. 2 vols. London: Macmillan, 1893.

Jensen, Christian, ed. *Hyperidis Orationes Sex cum Ceterarum Fragmentis*. Leipzig: Teubner, 1917.

Kennedy, George. *The Art of Rhetoric in the Roman World*. Princeton: Princeton University Press, 1972.

——. *Classical Rhetoric and Its Christian and Secular Tradition from Ancient to Modern Times*. Chapel Hill: University of North Carolina Press, 1980.

——. *Greek Rhetoric under Christian Emperors*. Princeton: Princeton University Press, 1983.

Kustas, George. *Studies in Byzantine Rhetoric*. Thessaloniki: Patriarchal Institute for Patristic Studies, 1973.

Lausberg, Heinrich. *Handbuch der Literarischen Rhetorik*. 2 vols. Munich: Max Hueber, 1960.

Lindberg, Gertrud. *Studies in Hermogenes and Eustathios: The Theory of Ideas and Its Application in the Commentaries of Eustathios on the Epics of Homer*. Lund: Lindell, 1977.

Maas, Paul. *Greek Metre*. Translated by Hugh Lloyd-Jones. Oxford: Clarendon Press, 1962.

Morrison, John Sinclair. "Antiphon." *Proceedings of the Cambridge Philological Society* 187 (1961) 49–58.

Nadeau, Ray. "Hermogenes *On Stases*: A Translation with an Introduction and Notes." *Speech Monographs* 31 (1964) 361–424.

Patterson, Annabel. *Hermogenes and the Renaissance: Seven Ideas of Style*. Princeton: Princeton University Press, 1970.

Rabe, Hugo. "Nachrichten über das Leben des Hermogenes." *Rheinisches Museum* 62 (1907) 247–262.

——, ed. *Hermogenis Opera*. Leipzig: Teubner, 1913.

——, ed. *Syriani in Hermogenem Commentaria*, I. Leipzig: Teubner, 1892.

Rowe, Galen. "Demosthenes' Use of Language." In *Demosthenes' On the Crown*, edited by James Murphy, 175–199. New York: Random House, 1967.

Russell, Donald. *Greek Declamation*. Cambridge: Cambridge University Press, 1983.

———— and Michael Winterbottom, eds. *Ancient Literary Criticism: The Principal Texts in New Translations*. Oxford: Clarendon Press, 1972.

Spengel, Leonard, ed. *Rhetores Graeci*. 3 vols. Leipzig: Teubner, 1853–56.

Walz, Christian, ed. *Rhetores Graeci*. 9 vols. London, 1832–36. Reprinted Osnabruck: Otto Zeller, 1968.

Wooten, Cecil. *Cicero's Philippics and Their Demosthenic Model: The Rhetoric of Crisis*. Chapel Hill: University of North Carolina Press, 1983.

Index of Passages Cited

All page references are to Rabe's pages.

Index of Topics and Names

Index of Technical Terms